I view with great delight the release of *Miracle Invasion*. Cycles of awakening are always needed, whether in a local congregation, a faithful leader, or a believing saint. I pray God will ignite us all through this book about the miraculous gifts of the Spirit.

—JACK HAYFORD, chancellor emeritus, The King's University;
past president, The Foursquare Church; founding pastor
of The Church on the Way (Van Nuys, CA)

Perhaps you've wondered if miracles still happen today or doubted their existence altogether. Maybe you've relegated miracles to something that occurs only in faraway lands and in different cultures. If so, then *Miracle Invasion* is a must-read. God is desperate to show you just how big, how wide, and how deep his love for you is. This book will give you eyes to see his kind, thoughtful, wonderful, and yes, miraculous plan for your life.

—SAMUEL RODRIGUEZ, president,
National Hispanic Christian Leadership Conference

Miracle Invasion has been written right on time. The Holy Spirit's power to infuse our present, broken world with the exact prescription for restoring life and hope is clearly evidenced in this profound report. I was particularly struck by a statement in the "Introduction," where Jeff Farmer says, "we were smitten with wonder." I believe that in this time of global cynicism, fear, and doubt, we must again be shaken to our core by the Lord's almighty power until we are smitten with wonder!

—GLENN C. BURRIS, Jr., president, The Foursquare Church

Since the day of Pentecost, Holy Spirit-inspired miracles have characterized those who walk in the full gospel message. In a rationalistic age that shows the limits of human imagination and ingenuity, this collection of documented miracles will inspire all of us to a greater walk of faith and expectation.

—DOUGLAS Pᵣᵢ...   ent, International
Holiness Church

This book shows God's miracle hand constantly reaching out to those who call on him. Believers must know we are protected by his Spirit, watching over us and waiting to help us every step of the way. We can trust God; his supernatural provision will see us through.

—CHARLES E. BLAKE, Sr., presiding bishop, Church of God in Christ; senior pastor, West Angeles COGIC (Los Angeles)

In a world enthralled with superheroes and spiritual phenomena, *Miracle Invasion* offers a clear, authenticated picture of the true source of supernatural power for those hungering for something more. Since we are narrative beings who love a story, this book offers solid teaching in a captivating way that will impact all generations and cultures.

—KAY HORNER, executive director, Awakening America Alliance

Critical to our twenty-first-century gospel witness is the Acts 2:12 inquiry, "What does this mean?" Only as we can give Peter's reply that "this is that" spoken of by our Lord in his Word do we have a platform for gospel transformation. This timely account of his work among twenty-first-century followers encourages us as laborers to enter his harvest with confident faith that he is the author of miracles!

—DAVID FERGUSON, executive director, Great Commandment Network

It is wonderful to read scriptural accounts in the early church of unfettered faith, miracles, and manifestations of power. But my cry today is that of Gideon's: "Where are all the miracles that our fathers told us about?" (Judges 6:13). *Miracle Invasion* contains stories about people whose experiences testify to contemporary miracles like our fathers told us about. May your faith be freshly stimulated.

—RANDALL A. BACH, president, Open Bible Church

I find myself praying for leaders and followers of Jesus to have a "gift of faith" as they face tasks and callings that are overwhelming. I believe with them that God will do that which is above and beyond what we are asking or thinking. The book *Miracle Invasion* will affirm and inspire those of us who are expecting the above and beyond that God is desiring to do in our lives and ministries. My encouragement is: Read it, live it!

—David Wells, general superintendent,
Pentecostal Assemblies of Canada

Filled with true stories of Holy Spirit power and miracles in our generation, this book will stir your heart and increase your faith.

—Robert B. Fort, chairman, United Evangelical Churches

After a long journey with Alzheimer's, my dad lay in a catatonic state, having not made a sound for four months. Mom was emotionally, physically, and spiritually depleted. However, Dad miraculously revived and preached one final sermon. He declared to Mom, "You know what, honey? God still answers prayer." If, like my mother, you need your hope restored, read *Miracle Invasion,* and you will be convinced that miracles still happen today!

—Alton Garrison, assistant general superintendent,
Assemblies of God USA

The gifts of the Holy Spirit are still in operation today! *Miracle Invasion* will increase your faith and give you an expectancy of what the Holy Spirit can do in your church, community, family, and ministry.

—Shannon Truelove, overseer/bishop,
International Pentecostal Church of Christ

MIRACLE INVASION

Amazing true
stories of the
Holy Spirit's gifts
at work today

Dean Merrill

BroadStreet
PUBLISHING

BroadStreet Publishing® Group, LLC
Savage, Minnesota USA
BroadStreetPublishing.com

MIRACLE INVASION:
Amazing true stories of the Holy Spirit's gifts at work today

ISBN-13: 978-1-4245-5608-3 (softcover)
ISBN-13: 978-1-4245-5609-0 (e-book)

All Scripture quotations, unless otherwise indicated, are taken from the Holy Bible, New International Version. Copyright © 1973, 1978, 1984, 2011 by Biblica, Inc. Used by permission of Biblica, Inc. All rights reserved worldwide. Scripture quotations marked MEV are taken from the Modern English Version (MEV). Copyright © 2014 by Military Bible Association. Used by permission. All rights reserved. Scriptures marked NKJV are taken from the New King James Version. Copyright© 1982 by Thomas Nelson, Inc. Used by permission. All rights reserved. Scripture quotations marked WEB are taken from the World English Bible, public domain. Scripture quotations marked KJV are taken from the King James Version, public domain.

Stock or custom editions of BroadStreet Publishing titles may be purchased in bulk for educational, business, ministry, fundraising, or sales promotional use. For information, please email info@broadstreet publishing.com.

Cover design by Chris Garborg at garborgdesign.com
Typesetting by Katherine Lloyd at theDESKonline.com

Printed in the United States of America
18 19 20 21 22 5 4 3 2 1

"… so that the works of God
might be displayed …"

John 9:3

CONTENTS

SETTING THE STAGE

Foreword by Jeff Farmer, president,
Pentecostal/Charismatic Churches of North America

Mother's Thanksgiving table was picture-perfect. Her lavish centerpiece glowed with hues of autumn color. Great-grandmother's antique silverware flanked our beautiful Lenox china. The turkey, encompassed by a moat of green parsley and laced with lavender plums, was golden brown. The mashed potatoes and gravy, green beans, and sweet potatoes were hot and ready to serve.

Everyone was there: Mom and Dad, my older sister, my younger brother … and of course, me. Nothing could ruin this moment. Nothing, that is, until Dad tried to sit down. For six months he had suffered with disabling back pain. Every morning he slipped into a steel brace hoping to mollify the chronic suffering. He couldn't even drive a car unless his custom-made board seat was placed on the cushion beneath the steering wheel.

This unforgettable holiday was the first time I saw a grown man cry. As Dad started to sit, he got stuck in a partially seated position. The pain was so severe he couldn't finish sitting down; yet he couldn't stand back up. His desperate cry frightened us all. By the time we got Dad into bed, Thanksgiving was pretty much ruined.

Afterward, the rest of us ate the delicious meal and prepared for dessert when Mom shouted, "Oops! I forgot the whipped cream for the pumpkin pie!" She promptly elected me to rush to the QuikTrip just two blocks away. It would be open on this holiday. With the Cool Whip in hand, I paid the clerk, got back into my tan and white '55 Chevy, and drove home.

Miracles Today?

A miracle healing for my dad was not on the radar, and far out of range for our family's worldview back then in the midsixties. My life was pretty much defined by girls, grades, and sports. All of my needs were cared for by my parents, and the closest I came to the supernatural was Clark Kent leaping tall buildings and flying faster than speeding bullets.

I did go to church, but it was a liberal Protestant congregation. People became Christians, they said, by taking a pastor's class and getting baptized. When my sister decided to join, I agreed to follow. Coming out of the baptismal tank, they gave me a certificate of church membership and told me I was a Christian. Nothing could have been further from the truth.

Nineteen sixty-three was the year Mom and Dad had been invited to hear a man named Larry Hammond talk about an amazing physical healing he had experienced. I really don't think Dad would have gone, except that the speaker had a PhD. My father valued education and couldn't reconcile medical science with miracles. So he was curious. Mom, on the other hand, was thirsting for truth … and for God.

Dr. Hammond's extraordinary testimony of an instantaneous, hospital deathbed healing in response to prayer rocked my parents' world. Dad wanted more information, and that meant connecting with people—lots of people. Our home turned into Grand Central Station, thrusting the Farmer family into a strange world of unfamiliar faces, gospel music instead of sacred hymns, and prayer meetings where people raised their hands in worship and prayed out loud all at the same time.

These exuberant believers talked about miracles as casually as I did about Friday night dances and the latest Elvis hit. To me, their stories sounded strange, even impossible to believe—until that Thanksgiving Day when I walked through the door of our home on Boston Street in Wichita, Kansas, and encountered the living, miracle-working God.

First Miracle

As I entered our home, my dad—the one we had half-dragged and half-carried to bed—was doing jumping jacks and deep knee bends in the kitchen. "I'm healed! I'm healed!" he shouted at the top of his lungs. His face was glowing. Mom was crying.

"What … what happened?" I asked, picking my jaw up off the floor.

"I was listening to a tape the Coxes gave me," he explained, referring to the family who had invited us to their church. "The preacher on the tape said, 'If you're listening to this message through a taped recording, reach out and touch the recorder as a point of faith. Good! Now, ask God to heal you.'"

Desperate and hopeful, Dad had done just that while I was down the street getting Cool Whip. "It was like a warm heating pad touched my back," Dad exclaimed. "I felt it! God delivered and healed me. I'm free! The pain is gone."

We sat down for dessert, overcome with awe. As newcomers to this kind of faith, we were smitten with wonder. That day marked me forever, teaching me an important truth—someone with a personal experience is never at the mercy of someone with an argument! A miracle settles every quarrel over the reality of God and the authenticity of his Word.

More than fifty years have now passed. Since then, I have witnessed more miracles and manifestations of the gifts of the Spirit than I can remember. And every time God displays his power and glory, I am humbled and awed to see beyond the veil.

The Natural and the Spiritual

"What veil?" you ask. I'm talking about the veil that separates the natural from the spiritual. Let me explain.

Jesus told the woman at the well that "God is spirit."[1] When God created people in the very beginning, he made them in his image and likeness, as spirit beings.[2] When he fashioned us outwardly, however, he gave us a natural body.[3] Therefore, a dynamic tension is ever-present between the spiritual and natural.

Miracles and the other gifts of the Spirit have their origin in the spirit dimension. They are beyond natural—they are *super*natural. They are spiritual. They are otherworldly because their source of authority and power originates outside of this natural world.

Unless a person is born again by the Spirit of God (by grace through faith in Jesus Christ), he or she does not understand this unseen reality. That is why a skeptic, or anyone who rejects Christ, has trouble admitting that miracles take place. Their natural mind cannot apprehend the things of the Spirit.[4] In fact, modern-day miracles are foolishness to them.

Opposition and rejection of things of the Spirit go beyond unbelievers, however. Many Christians also struggle with the spirit dimension, often because they have not experienced the power associated with being baptized in the Holy Spirit, as recorded at least four times in the New Testament.[5]

Even some church leaders are afraid of the moving of the Spirit. They are unfamiliar with his person, his works, and his gifts. They are more comfortable in the natural arena and are strangers to the realm of the supernatural. Leaders can control natural events, but the Holy Spirit cannot be controlled, organized, or duplicated. And he is full of surprises!

When the Holy Spirit came upon the 120 followers of Jesus Christ at Pentecost,[6] he took everyone by surprise. Is it any wonder, then, that his miraculous actions today are still a surprise?

Manifestations of the miraculous gifts of the Spirit have their origin in a real spiritual dimension and cannot be analyzed in our intellectual laboratories or voted upon in our church committees. Only the Spirit of God "knows" the things of God.[7]

Many church leaders don't want surprises during their worship services. So, authentic manifestations of the Spirit have diminished in number, at least in churches of the West. Sadly, we are more comfortable trying to fit God into our dimension of the natural rather than rising in faith to trust his power and glory in the dimension of the spiritual.

Supernatural Action through Gifts of the Spirit

However, the message of Scripture is clear: The miraculous nature of God is to be seen at work through his children. God has provided for supernatural acts and events to take place through his sons and daughters by the gifts of the Spirit.

It is true, some miracles God initiates by himself without any involvement of people: he dispatches an angel to save a life,[8] ignites a desert bush into a fiery ball without it being consumed,[9] or strikes down the persecutor of the infant church with a flash of lightning that renders him blind.[10] These are sovereign acts of God, requiring no participation by people—they are miracles.

Other miracles, however, are the result of men, women, and even children stepping out in bold reliance on the Word of God. The Holy Spirit equips and anoints them with a *charisma* ("grace-gift") and sets in motion a supernatural event that is beyond any power or resource of mankind. The result is not a coincidence of circumstances and is completely unexplainable to the natural mind. That is to say, the miracle is unreasonable.

Paul, the great apostle of the first-century church, provided three gift lists in the Bible.[11] These lists describe assorted gifts distributed to believers through which the Holy Spirit moves to administer the church and usher in the kingdom of God. The testimonies and miracle stories you are about to read in this book spotlight the list found in 1 Corinthians 12 and illustrate that when one of these nine gifts of the Spirit is in operation, it is nothing short of a miracle.

"There are various gifts, but the same Spirit." (1 Corinthians 12:4 MEV)

"To one is given by the Spirit the word of wisdom, to another the word of knowledge by the same Sprit, to another faith by the same Spirit, to another gifts of healing by the same Spirit, to another the working of miracles, to another prophecy, to another discerning of spirits, to another various kinds of tongues, and to another the interpretation of tongues." (1 Corinthians 12:8–10 MEV)

Before we read these stories, let's take a brief look into the gifts that will be featured throughout this book. Here, the nine gifts are divided into three categories: revelatory gifts (word of knowledge, word of wisdom, and discerning of spirits), power gifts (faith, gifts of healing, and working of miracles), and inspiration gifts (various kinds of tongues, interpretation of tongues, and prophecy). These categories provide deeper insight into the gifts and further explain the faith by which each gift operates. Understanding these differences also allows us to see just how impactful and powerful a miracle can be when two gifts, from two different categories, work in tandem. Included at the end of each gift section are examples from the early church. These examples are excellent resources you can use for further study into the gifts.

Revelatory Gifts

Revelation is the self-disclosure of God—divine enablements to know what God knows. As the Holy Spirit wills, that which God knows can be revealed to us as a gift of the Spirit. Scripture says, "Now we have received … the Spirit who is from God, that we might know" (1 Corinthians 2:12 NKJV). These three gifts provide supernatural understanding to know something presently unknown.

Word of Knowledge

The word of knowledge is a supernatural, Holy Spirit revelation of facts or information known by God. It does not draw upon knowledge acquired by academic study or experience. It is not enhanced human knowledge or natural enlightenment. Rather, it is knowledge miraculously revealed to one of God's children by the Holy Spirit. For instance, God could reveal the location of a missing person or of something lost. He might reveal the location of an event or the cause of a sickness. The word of knowledge is supernatural insight revealing specific information about a person, place, or thing and may come to the believer through a mental impression, picture, dream, or vision.

Early church example: Peter exposed the lie of how much money Ananias and Sapphira said they received from their land sale (Acts 5:1–11).

Word of Wisdom

The word of wisdom, listed in the Bible first among the nine spiritual gifts, is supernatural revelation by the Spirit of how to rightly apply knowledge. In its highest form, it is an expression of divine purpose of the mind and will of God. The word of wisdom has been employed, for example, to warn of approaching danger or conflict; to make known a divine call to service in the kingdom; to apprise of coming judgment or blessing; to give counsel in problem solving or personal guidance in special circumstances; or to reveal the future. The tandem gifts of the word of knowledge and word of wisdom can have significant impact in building the church as they supply supernatural understanding of the will and purpose of God. Whereas the information revealed in a word of knowledge relates to the past or present, a word of wisdom usually points to the future.

Early church example: James, the Lord's brother, resolved the Jew/Gentile tension at the Jerusalem Council and set the course for ongoing church expansion (Acts 15:13–21).

Discerning of Spirits

Discerning of spirits gives supernatural insight into the unseen realm of spirits. There are three kinds of spirits: divine (heavenly), satanic (devilish), and human—not a person's disposition or personality, but the highest part of one's three-part being.[12] By this gift, a believer may know the origin of any spirit(ual) manifestation. This is much more than simply keen perception or psychological insight; rather, this gift often partners with one of the power gifts (working of miracles, faith, gifts of healings) to deliver people who are afflicted, tormented, or oppressed by the Devil. This gift brings hope for liberation, healing, and freedom. It also discloses error and unmasks servants of Satan.

Early church examples: Peter deals with Simon the sorcerer (Acts 8:9–24), and Paul deals with the false prophet Bar-Jesus/Elymas (Acts 13:6–12) and with the fortune-teller girl in Philippi (Acts 16:16–18).

Power Gifts

In serving the Lord and serving people, it is often insufficient merely to know; we must also be able to do. These three gifts impart supernatural ability to act in obedience to faith. Through the power gifts, the Holy Spirit supernaturally empowers believers to act according to God's purpose. The results are grand, miraculous displays of God's glory and power.

Faith

Distinct from saving faith[13] or the fruit of the Spirit,[14] the gift of faith is considered by many the greatest of the three power gifts. (Note: the "fruit" of faith/faithfulness is for our character; the "gift" of faith is for releasing God's power.) Unlike the other gifts that represent miraculous *acts* of the Spirit, the gift of faith is more a *process* of the Spirit. It is a supernatural impartation aligned with the will of God (and often spoken by a servant of God) that shall come to pass in the future. Through this gift the Spirit gives resolve and power to believe for the impossible in the face of difficult circumstances. It often results in a divine deposit of peace and confidence for believers.

Early church example: Paul declares in the midst of a typhoon that no lives would be lost (Acts 27:33–37, 44).

Gifts of Healings

These gifts (plural in the original Greek) are for supernatural healings of diseases and infirmities. Healings through these gifts are by the power of the Holy Spirit without human aid. They do not imply assistance or intervention by medical professionals (physicians, surgeons, and so forth), however grateful we are for them. The Lord Jesus had compassion on the sick and exercised these gifts frequently throughout his public ministry. He also commanded his disciples to "heal the sick."[15] In Scripture, these gifts operated in various ways—for instance, through a word, by the laying on of hands, by an apostle's passing shadow, by a piece of fabric, or by anointing with oil.

Early church examples: The lame beggar is healed at the temple gate (Acts 3:1–10); blind Saul of Tarsus receives his sight (Acts 9:10–19); and Aeneas the cripple in Lydda walks again (Acts 9:32–35).

Working of Miracles

A miracle is an event that supersedes known scientific, natural laws, which are temporarily suspended because of a supernatural act of God. "The working of miracles," according to Bible teacher Fuchsia Pickett in her 2004 trilogy on the Holy Spirit,[16] is literally rendered "operations of supernatural powers" in the Greek. Clearly, all nine gifts of the Spirit are miracles, so what is unique about this gift? It refers exclusively to acts of power and would exclude demonstrations of power identified in the other gifts. A healing miracle, for instance, is a case of the gifts of healing. However, with the working of miracles, the Spirit gives authority to a servant of the Lord to display explosions of God's supernatural omnipotence (unlimited power) for the purpose of intervening and counteracting earthly and evil forces.

Early church examples: Three different occasions where apostles were released from prison in the middle of the night (Acts 5:19–20; 12:1–10; 16:22–40); two separate stories of apostles resurrecting someone from the dead (Acts 9:36–42; 20:7–12); and Paul surviving being bitten by a poisonous snake (Acts 28:3–6).

Inspiration Gifts

Inspiration gifts are often also called vocal or voice gifts. Whereas revelatory gifts cause us to *know,* and power gifts move us to *do,* gifts of inspiration anoint us to *speak.* The Holy Spirit has designed these gifts as tools to inspire, edify, exhort, and correct. They build the church and inspire people. Each of the inspiration gifts is a display of supernatural utterance.

Various Kinds of Tongues

This gift does not refer to the tongue(s) or prayer language(s) given to a believer at the initial baptism in the Holy Spirit.[17] When uttering a prayer language, a person is speaking to God, not people, and therefore the tongue does not require interpretation. On the other hand, the gift of the Spirit referenced in 1 Corinthians 12 is given for the edification of the church and must be interpreted in the language of those present.[18] The gift of speaking in tongues is a supernatural utterance, prompted by the Spirit, in a language never learned by the speaker. It is not understood by the speaker and in most cases is not understood by the hearer. Jesus acknowledged this gift as for "those who believe."[19] Edification is always the test for this gift's proper use.[20]

Early church example: Instructions to the Corinthian church on speaking in tongues (1 Corinthians 14:26–27).

Interpretation of Tongues

Interpretation of tongues is the follow-up interpretation of an utterance in tongues in a public service. The interpreter does not understand the exact words of the tongue spoken, and hence is not *translating* what was said, but rather *interprets* by the Spirit what God is communicating in the message. The interpreter is to explain thoroughly what was spoken in tongues, not translate. This explains why sometimes the interpretation is longer or shorter than the message in tongues. The interpretation is just as much a miracle as the tongues themselves. Those who speak in other tongues are admonished to pray for the ability to interpret,[21] so the church may be edified if no other interpreter is present. The one possessing this gift makes utterances of tongues understandable in the common language of those present.

Early church example: Instructions to the Corinthian church on interpreting tongues (1 Corinthians 14:26–28).

Prophecy

Scripture specifically commands us to "desire"[22] this gift and states plainly that everyone may prophesy.[23] Prophecy is an in-the-moment, unrehearsed, divinely inspired, supernatural, anointed message. Many Christians unfortunately fail to distinguish between the office of the prophet[24] and the gift of prophecy. Both are referred to as gifts in Scripture, but the office is an ongoing gift of Christ to his church, and the spiritual endowment is a gift of the Spirit to an individual. To give an utterance with prophetic anointing is altogether different than giving an educated prediction. Prophecy is for the purpose of edification, exhortation, and comfort.[25] It is a Spirit-empowered declaration that could include prediction of the future (foretelling) as well as proclamation of divine purpose (forth-telling). All true prophecy exalts Jesus and edifies the church.

Early church examples: Agabus prophesied on several occasions (Acts 11:27–28; 21:10–11) and instructions to the Roman church (Romans 12:6), the Corinthian church (1 Corinthians 14:29–32, 39), and the Thessalonian church (1 Thessalonians 5:19–22) regarding the gift of prophecy.

With this foundation of the gifts in mind, and a grasp of the Holy Spirit's design by which they operate, we can now embrace them and rejoice in the following true, credible, authentic examples of the gifts of the Spirit ministering in *our* time across *our* continent.

These are amazing true stories of God at work today. Our colleagues, neighbors, and friends were eyewitnesses to these miracles. They will inspire you and give you hope in the midst of your own difficult circumstances. And I pray they will encourage you to step out in faith and obey the Spirit's promptings when he anoints *you* to know, to do, and to say.

chapter 1

UP FROM
A WATERY GRAVE

Is this story an example of the gift of extraordinary faith?[1] Or does it display the working of miracles?[2] Perhaps a combination of both.

Whatever the case, this remarkable account (condensed from a posting on PE News by coeditor Dan Van Veen) showcases the Spirit's intervention at a desperate hour.

For many St. Louis-area children, January 19, 2015, was a day off from school in honor of Martin Luther King Jr. Day. But for fourteen-year-old John Smith, the fun day with his friends quickly turned tragic. The weather had turned unseasonably warm. John and two basketball teammates—both named Josh—decided to venture out onto frozen Lake Saint Louis, which lies west of the city. They were not thinking about the fact that the farther they got from shore, the thinner the ice would become.

About 150 feet out, John suddenly fell through the ice. His friend Josh Sander tried to grab his hand, but the ice broke under him. Josh Rieger, the third boy, then tried lying on his stomach to reach his friends, but the ice gave way under him as well. His sister, Jamie Rieger, watched from the shore in horror as cries of "Call 9-1-1!" echoed across the lake.

By the time Lake Saint Louis Fire and Water Rescue arrived, Josh Sander was pulling himself onto land, while Josh Rieger clung to the ice edge in the lake. Deploying quickly, they rescued him. But, where was John Smith?

"He's under the ice!" the others shouted. By now, fifteen minutes had passed. No longer was John flailing his arms in a final and terrifying attempt to stay afloat. His lungs were filled with raw lake water, his heart had stopped beating, and he lay motionless on the bottom. He had lost his battle for life.

Wentzville firefighter, Tommy Shine, kept probing the icy water with a recovery pole in hopes of finding the boy's body. After several vain attempts, he sensed someone—Someone?—telling him, *Move two steps to the left.* When he did so, the pole's hook immediately snagged John's clothing. The firefighter pulled John's lifeless body to the surface.

A Doctor's Notes

Within seconds, the ambulance was racing toward St. Joseph Hospital West in the city of Lake Saint Louis, where Dr. Kent Sutterer was on call. He searched in vain for a pulse. His expectations, after this much time under water, were grim at best.

The boy's mother, Joyce Smith, came dashing into the waiting area while CPR attempts continued for another twenty-seven minutes. Finally it was time—after close to an hour since John had fallen through the ice—to face the fact that he was gone. Dr. Sutterer called the mother into the room, ready to record an official time of death.

"I didn't realize what he was preparing to do," Joyce remembers. "I just knew we were in dire need of God. The doctor said I could touch John, so I walked up to his bed, grabbed his feet, and started praying that God would send his Holy Spirit to raise him up and heal him.

"And within moments of praying, they got a pulse!"

Joyce says the surprise on everyone's faces was obvious. They jumped into a flurry of action; a large young man resumed CPR. Dr. Sutterer, whose own daughter was a classmate of John's at Living Word Christian Middle School, wrote a notation immediately afterward that best tells the facts:

I had exhausted all interventions in my scientific armamentarium without even a hint of success. All the resources of this world were being thrust upon this young man with no indication except the cold reality of a young life snuffed out before our very eyes.

But the interventions of modern medicine are not what John's mother was counting on. "Spiritual warfare" is what she called this. No sooner did John's mother call on the Holy Spirit to bring her son back to her than the monitor started [a] rhythmic beat, [while] a pulse could be felt in his groin and his carotid artery. ...

I don't know that John Smith will ever be the same as he was before he fell through the ice. But I know that God can do more than we ever imagined. I know that God has given us a gift, even if it is only for a few days. I was privileged to witness a miracle.

I was preparing myself to give a mother the final bad news that her son was gone from this world. She had more faith in God than I did. She called on God, and God brought him back. ... The Holy Spirit came in that room [and] started that boy's heart once again.

With his heart now beating, John was quickly transported to Cardinal Glennon Children's Medical Center in the heart of Saint Louis. The doctor on staff was Dr. Jeremy Garrett, who happened to be an expert in dealing with water-accident victims.

After examining John, he called the family in. "He told us John had only brain stem activity, that his lungs were full of acid, and that if he did live, he would be a vegetable," Joyce Smith recalls. Garrett then asked about a DNR ("do not resuscitate") order.

The brave mother shook her head. "Doctor, I understand that you're the best," she replied. "Do the best of your ability—the rest is up to God."

Rallying the Prayer Team

By now her husband, Brian, had arrived, as well as their pastor, Jason Noble, of First Assembly Church, in the suburb of Saint Peter. Other pastors from the area had come as well. "We went to John's room and started praying," Pastor Noble recalls. "He was totally unresponsive. We prayed for about ten minutes—and then I saw two angels appear, like guardians! The moment I saw them, John suddenly squeezed my hand and opened his eyes."

Just as quickly, however, the boy closed his eyes and fell asleep. The group renewed their prayer efforts, asking specifically that God would fill John's lungs with new breath and restore his brain.

"I was praying up by John's head, whispering into his ear," the pastor says, "when suddenly I saw thousands of whirling, colorful lights around his head, like they were rewiring John's brain. I told the others in the room what I was seeing, but they couldn't see it.

"And then John sat up in his bed, eyes wide open, and grabbed my hand!"

For the next week, Pastor Noble continued his bedside prayer vigil every day, starting at eight a.m. The doctors tested John's lungs, expecting to find rampant and intense infection due to the intake of raw, dirty lake water. But the test came back sterile.

The acidosis had originally measured at 6.6 pH level (normal is between 7.35 and 7.45)—the Smiths still have the X-rays and test reports to prove it. The lowest level that can sustain life was said to be 6.8. Yet John was not only alive but alert enough to respond to Dr. Garrett's questions, despite the ventilator in his mouth. With his hands he indicated the right answers about his favorite two basketball players, LeBron James and Michael Jordan.

"Every day, John made huge improvement," the pastor says. "In a little over a week, he was taken off the ventilator and could start talking."

The news spread throughout the hospital. The desperate parents of a young boy in the next room named Jackson sought out Joyce Smith. Their son was paralyzed head to toe from the flu; plus, he had a serious infection. "They saw all the people in the waiting room praying for John," Pastor Noble recalls, "and they begged Joyce to pray for their son too. People were glad to do so. By that night, the boy was sitting up in bed, singing. Soon, the paralysis was totally gone!"

After just sixteen days, John Smith walked out of the hospital completely recovered. He even visited his school to thank everyone for praying for him and to pick up his homework.

Not long afterward, Living Word Christian Middle School had a guest evangelist speak at its Thursday morning chapel service. "He gave a strong salvation message," says Nancy Benes, the principal, "and about a hundred children made salvation decisions or rededicated their lives to Christ. I know at least some of those decisions were related to John's experience, because I asked them."

Visitors that day in the chapel service were watching too. One parent as well as a kitchen worker raised their hands to accept Christ along with the students. "It's awesome to see the ripple effect of God's miraculous work in John's life," says the pastor.

Churches and the school have in fact taken action to keep the ripples moving. They printed T-shirts that say ASK ME ABOUT JOHN SMITH in order to elicit more sharing opportunities.

And John himself has seen God work in others' lives. He texted an atheist friend of the family who lives in Germany about the miracles he had experienced. The friend texted back, "For the first time I have prayed to God. I have chicken skin [goose bumps]!"

Says John's mom, "I believe God is raising up a generation and showing them his might so they will trust him and proclaim him as God. He also wants us to know that he cares for us. The word that God is speaking right now is: When you seek my face and come to me, I will do great and marvelous things for you!"

To watch the local TV news coverage of John's resurrection, go to: http://www.ksdk.com/news/teen-who-fell-in-icy -pond-makes-miraculous-recovery/211167177.

chapter 2

SUBWAY AND WALMART

Sometimes a word of knowledge comes not in sentences but in pictures.

Brian Sawyer, a Pentecostal Holiness missions director, had stopped more than once to get a quick sandwich at the Subway shop in Edenton, North Carolina. He had come to know the young man behind the counter who made his buffalo chicken favorite, chatting comfortably about how his day was going and where Brian's recent travels had taken him.

"So what were you doing this time?" the employee asked one day, referring to the most recent destination.

"Just talking to people about the Lord," Brian replied. "He wants everybody to know that he cares about them and loves them, you know. Sometimes he speaks to me and tells me what's going on in their lives."

"That's cool!" the young man said. By then, the sandwich was completed and ready for payment. Brian sat down at a table to eat, across from an adjacent table where a short, dark-haired young woman sat—the employee's twenty-something girlfriend, in jeans and a T-shirt. They quickly began conversing.

"What is it you do?" she asked.

Brian gave a quick summary of his work. When he mentioned hearing from God, she interjected, "Well, you know, it's interesting that you say that—because one time I was driving down a road, and for some reason, I had this overwhelming thought that I should turn and go a different way. I turned—not knowing until later that there was a big wreck farther down the way I would normally drive. What do you think? Was that God speaking to me?"

"Could very well be!" Brian answered. "A lot of times God is trying to direct our lives even if we don't know it."

Just then, while looking into the young woman's face, he saw in his mind's eye something superimposed in front of her on the table: a birthday cake with candles on top.

This wasn't the first time such an image had come his way. So he continued, "And you know what? It's kind of funny ... as I'm sitting here talking to you, I feel like God is showing me something. I'm seeing a birthday cake. Does that mean anything to you?"

Her eyes flew open with a start. "Oh my gosh!" she exclaimed. "Today is my brother's birthday, and as soon as I leave here, I'm going to go buy a cake for him!"

Brian, feeling encouraged by this, welcomed the next visual impression: an elderly woman who was obviously sick and, in fact, had her eyes closed. He then said, "And also ... I'm seeing an older lady who is maybe really important to you, and she has recently passed away ... and you're having a hard time with this."

Now the girl was shocked. "My grandmother ... she just passed away, like, this week," she said softly. Then without another word, she jumped up and made a beeline toward the restroom.

Her boyfriend at the cash register had been overhearing the conversation as he worked. Now he called out, "Dude! You just freaked her out!" Brian Sawyer could only shrug.

Questions

When the young woman returned in a minute or so, her face looked like she had seen a ghost. But she had processed the scene enough to determine that here was somebody in contact with the real God—which led her to sit again.

"Okay, I have some questions to ask you," she began. "I want to know what God thinks about the fact that I've been stealing underwear from this women's store over in the strip mall. Is that okay?"

Brian Sawyer held back any condemnation as he replied instead, "You know, God knows where you're at. He knows what you're going through. But you don't have to do that. If you ask God to provide for you, I believe he'll take care of your needs and will honor your decision not to steal."

He then pulled out his wallet and handed a twenty-dollar bill in her direction. "Here, take this," he said. "Use it to buy what you need."

"No, no, no!" she protested. "I can't take that from you."

"You're not taking anything," he replied. "I'm giving it to you; I'm wanting to bless you. Maybe this is God's way of helping you so you don't have do what you've been doing."

"I can't believe this!" she exclaimed, reluctantly accepting the money.

Soon she was on to a different topic. "Okay, I have another question. My boyfriend and I," she said, nodding toward the guy behind the counter, "really, really, really want to have a child. We've been trying and trying without success. I just wonder what God would think about this."

Again, Brian Sawyer restrained any impulse to lecture her. "Have you ever seen a bull's-eye, like they have on a bow-and-arrow shooting range?" he asked.

"Yes."

"Well, for you and him to have a baby at this point would be like hitting one of the outer rings on a target. But God has a prescribed way to do this that would be in the center of the bull's-eye. What is that way? To get married first and *then* have a child. That's what the Bible shows us. That's the way God can truly bless you two."

Standing up, she said, "Thank you so much. You've really made my day." She gave Brian a hug and was soon out the door while he left for his next appointment.

The Rest of the Story

Three or four years later, the Subway exchange in Edenton had been long forgotten as Brian stood in a Walmart checkout line thirty miles northeast in Elizabeth City. When there came a tap on his shoulder, he turned around to see a young mom with two little ones in her cart, plus she was pregnant.

"Hey, are you the guy who talked to me that one time about stealing," she asked with a quizzical look, "and then gave me money instead to pay for my clothes?"

"Uh ... I'm not sure," Brian replied, racking his memory. "I may be."

At that moment, her now-husband came up beside her. Seeing the two faces together flipped a switch in Brian's brain. "Yes! I remember you guys!"

"I just want to thank you for what you said that day," the woman explained. "It really changed my life. We listened to your advice, and we're married now." The conversation flew thick and fast after that, updating him on all that had blossomed in their lives. They introduced their two young children and told when the next one was due to be born.

On the way out to the parking lot, Brian Sawyer asked if they'd found a church. "We've been looking," they replied, "but with work schedules on Sunday and everything, we haven't quite got that figured out yet."

"Well, you might want to check out my church—Fountain of Life. It's just a couple of miles down this road, and we have a Sunday night service that might fit for you guys."

"Oh, yes—we know where that is!" they replied. "We'll see."

Says Brian Sawyer in reflection, "You never know what impact you might make on another person. So if you get the chance to interact with someone, no matter where you are … slow down. Listen to what the Lord is saying or showing you and represent him to the best of your ability.

"There's a line in Romans 12 that says, 'If your gift is prophesying, then prophesy in accordance with your faith.'[1] We all need to step out in faith that God will lead us. Someone's life is depending on it."

chapter 3

A HIGHER CODE

David Killingsworth may have been the honored guest speaker that Sunday night at a multicultural church in Phoenix, but this didn't stop a humble Navajo lady from approaching him at the end of the service to prophesy. "The Lord is going to give you understanding and wisdom concerning the old ways of the Native people," she announced. "You will not get this from a book or a tape, but you will get it by revelation, because the Lord is going to use you to help redeem the culture and bring deliverance."

Pastor Killingsworth welcomed this message in light of his ongoing interest in reaching Native Americans. His church, Green Forest Christian Center[1] back in northwest Arkansas, had already sent several work and outreach teams to the small reservation town of Jeddito, Arizona, a Navajo enclave within the Hopi tribe's larger territory. The town had a small log cabin church building where various groups had tried over the years to start a congregation without success.

The pastor flew home that Monday. When he showed up at his office the next day, a staff member reported, "There was a missionary on sabbatical who stopped by the Sunday night prayer meeting; after we had all prayed for a while, he said, 'I have a word from the Lord for the father of this house.' We told him, 'Well, he's not here; he's in Arizona.'"

The visitor was not dissuaded. He asked if they might tape his message, to be played when the senior pastor returned. They accommodated him by bringing out a cassette recorder.

Now at his desk, Pastor Killingsworth sat down to listen. He punched the Play button and began to hear the following words: "The Lord says, 'I will give you understanding and wisdom concerning the old ways of the Native people. You will not get this by book or by tape, but you will get it by revelation. And I will use you to redeem the culture and bring deliverance.'" It was virtually the identical message he had been given 1,200 miles west at essentially the same hour back on Sunday night.

In response, "Our church began to pray ever more seriously about this over the next period of time," says the pastor. "We kept up our connections to Navajo people we'd already met and tried to extend our network. We came to believe God wanted us to try again to plant a church in Jeddito."

And so it was that in August 2001, a team of some fifteen Green Forest people, including committed intercessors, came to the town once again to pray for a spiritual awakening. Several Navajo believers from Phoenix joined them, asking God to break through the dark superstitions of the culture with the light of the gospel. During one prayer meeting, a woman in her sixties, named Judy Magner, began to bear down in urgent entreaty, interceding in a flow of tongues.

"I noticed two Navajo ladies softly weeping nearby," the pastor recalls. "It struck me as unusual, since Navajo people are known to be restrained and unemotional."

After some minutes, Judy gradually quieted herself. The observing ladies said to the pastor, "Where did she get to know our language?"

David Killingsworth chuckled as he replied, "I can assure you—Judy only knows how to speak 'Texan!' She's hardly mastered proper English."

"No, no," the ladies protested. "She's been praying in Navajo for probably the last ten minutes."

Navajo is a complex, tonal language and is well-known to be one of the most difficult languages on earth—so hard that during World War II the US Marines enlisted up to five hundred bilingual Navajos to pass classified tactical messages back and forth across the Pacific. The Japanese enemy forces never did crack their code.

What was even more remarkable was the content of Judy's prayer. "She's been praying against the power of the 'skin-walker,'" the women said—a particular kind of Navajo medicine man who is said to be able to turn himself into (or disguise himself as) an animal, usually to bring harm to people. Many Navajos live in great fear of his powers.

Indeed, there was one of these men in the Jeddito community who had opposed every gospel effort up to this time. Now within sixty days, this "skin-walker" abruptly moved away. The church plant proceeded unhindered, becoming a healthy gathering of Christian believers, as Pastor Killingsworth and his teams kept coming every month for the next year and a half. Navajos—especially young people—were saved and filled with the Spirit in a genuine season of revival.

The work was eventually handed over to a nearby missionary to continue. Meanwhile, the pastor from Arkansas was "adopted" into the Navajo Nation and given a special name. Contact continues to this day. The little town has been a proving ground for the truth that "the one who is in you is greater than the one who is in the world."[2]

chapter 4

INSTANTLY

Of all the possible complications from diabetes—nerve pain, kidney problems, congestive heart failure, depression—perhaps the most devastating is blindness caused by bleeding in the retinas.

Andrea Anderson is a sweet, soft-spoken grandmother in Sarnia, Ontario, who tried her best to cope with her diabetes, until eventually, "Twelve years ago, I was having trouble seeing to the side," she relates. "So I went to the doctor about this.

"They gave me a test—and the next thing I knew, the doctor was saying I was legally blind!

"I was shocked. Within a week and a half, I had lost the sight in both eyes. I couldn't see the difference between light and darkness. There was nothing there—couldn't watch TV, couldn't tell the color of my clothing, or anything."

Plunged into a world of darkness, she made all the adjustments she could think of. Both the Red Cross and the March of Dimes lent their assistance. Friends picked her up for church. CNIB (Canadian National Institute for the Blind) taught her how to use a cane and also provided her with a "talking DAISY" machine that plays books from CDs. They sent a new CD on loan every month; the very first one provided was the Bible, which she was allowed to keep. Still, it was a grim existence day after day, month after month, year upon year.

Then Pentecost Sunday 2016 came to her church, Bethel Pentecostal. She will never forget that day. A visiting evangelist from West Virginia, named Ted Shuttlesworth, had been invited to minister. "It was a normal day," Andrea says; "it's always exciting and warm and Spirit-filled there. But that day, I don't know … it felt a little different.

"At the end of the morning service, Brother Ted asked for an altar call, and I went up. I wanted to pray for my little great-granddaughter, who was in the hospital. I was crying—I cry easily!

"Something led me to go back to church on Sunday night, even though I usually didn't go then. Brother Ted was going through the aisles, praying for people. All of a sudden, I felt a hand on the back of my head. He stopped and prayed for me.

"He didn't know me. I'd never spoken to him before."

Caught on Camera

To see what happened next, watch the video https://vimeo.com/196310250, starting at the 2:10 mark. The evangelist's prayer is short but commanding: "You blinding spirit, I command you to go and report to your master, Satan. You've failed in your mission to keep this woman blind. I command your eyes now to be healed and to begin to open. *Open*—for the glory of God!"

Within seconds, Andrea is up on her feet and following the speaker to the front of the church, where he puts her through a series of tests. She accurately follows his instructions from three feet away to do what he does: waving one hand back and forth, pointing upward with one finger, then two, then all five fingers, then stretching out her arm to the side, finally running in place.

By this point, the congregation of several hundred are on their feet erupting in praise to God. Andrea breaks down in tears of joy.

In the subsequent video interview, she opens into a wide smile as she reports, "My sight is good—it's good. I'm blessed. It's been fully restored."

Looking out the window, she adds, "I see the snow … I see the colors of the leaves, the trees blooming, the flowers coming out …

"My doctor was scratching his head. 'I'm scientific,' he said. 'I don't know what to say.' He looked again at all the reports of my coming to see him over the years, when I could see nothing. Now he put me through all kinds of tests, and I passed everything."

Her physician called in another doctor, saying, "This is the lady I was telling you about." On a return visit to the office, he added, "I've told my wife all about you. I've been telling other people too."

This kind of miracle, after more than a decade of documented blindness, is hard to refute. "I still have her white cane in my office at the church," says her pastor, Tim Gibb. "She obviously has no use for it anymore. This whole incident has been a great encouragement for our church and beyond, as the video has spread. It gives people hope that miracles really do happen."

chapter 5

DETOUR?

The first few times the Holy Spirit nudges a believer to exercise a spiritual gift, it's only natural to feel hesitant, as in *Really? I'm supposed to do WHAT? That's just "me" thinking up something, right? Or is this truly a God thing?*

Sterling Brackett, a nineteen-year-old college student from Tennessee Tech, was driving his gray Volkswagen Bug east on Interstate 40 toward his parents' place for the weekend when he thought the Lord said, *Get off at the next exit.*

Why? He was eager to get home on a Friday night after a long week of classes. The green signs for the next town of Crossville kept coming, but Sterling ignored them. He thought instead about the warm sights and smells of home that awaited him another forty minutes down the road.

Again, the inner voice spoke, *Well, you can be obedient, or you can be disobedient. What are you going to do?*

Chastised, he took the off-ramp, having no idea what would happen next. Before he reached the stop sign, the next directive seemed to come: *Take a right,* which led into the center of town. He kept driving until, once again, he heard, *Take a left.* He did so, soon to be given another, *Take a right,* which in a few blocks brought him to a stop in front of a mobile home.

Shutting off the engine, Sterling wondered what he should do next. After all, it was already dark. Was this neighborhood even safe? "I was apprehensive," he recalls, "but I couldn't escape the strong prompting of the Lord that I should go up to the door—and give them all my money!" This whole episode was getting stranger by the minute.

He knew good and well that all he had in his pocket was a dollar bill and some change. He had intended to use that for a little more gas, to ensure he didn't run out on the way. *Is this really the Lord,* he wondered, *or am I just going crazy?*

But Lord, I don't think I've got enough gas to get home, he protested.

I own the cattle on a thousand hills, the Lord responded. *And you're worried about getting home?*

Knocking on the Door

Taking a deep breath, the young student approached the mobile home door. A man in his late twenties opened it, peering out at the stranger on his step.

"Sir," Sterling began, "I was driving on the Interstate, and, um, the Lord directed me to your home. I don't know why. But he asked me to give you all of my money.

"And frankly, I'm embarrassed, because it's only this dollar bill and a few coins," he said, holding out his hand. "But it's all I have."

The man did not snicker or shut the door in Sterling's face. Rather, he immediately began to cry. "Come inside," he said through his tears.

Sterling walked in and sat down. The man began to explain. "The truth is, my wife is in bed already, and I've just put our baby girl to bed without a bottle. I've been sitting here feeling like an absolute failure for having nothing to provide. Now I can run down to the store and buy some milk, so I can wake her up and feed her!"

Both men stared at each other in amazement. The Holy Spirit had known what he was doing all along. The man said, "I realize now how important my family is to God."

They prayed together and then said goodbye. Sterling continued his homeward journey, arriving safely on just the gas he had. He even made it back to a gas station the following morning— once he, like any college student, had persuaded dear old mom to replenish his wallet.

Years later, news reached Sterling that the couple in the trailer had entered the ministry. Meanwhile, he went on to a lifetime in the Lord's service, eventually being named the Foursquare Church's corporate secretary and vice president of corporate affairs at the Los Angeles headquarters. But he's never forgotten what unfolded that dark Friday night in eastern Tennessee. "I felt almost like a bystander," he says today. "I just watched the Lord do what he had in mind, for a specific purpose known only to him. All I had to do was follow his leading."

chapter 6

JUST TEENAGERS

Lest anyone think spiritual gifts flow only through pastors, evangelists, and super-saints, consider the cases of two different youth groups—one in western Canada, the other in central United States—that illustrate what the Spirit can do through "just teenagers."

The Rolling Prayer Meeting

Fort McMurray, Alberta, sits far up in the northern forests—another 435 kilometers (270 miles) northeast of Edmonton, the provincial capital. But it's no sleepy outpost; it's the throbbing center of the Athabasca oil sands, where some 2 million barrels of petroleum are extracted every day—much of it headed to the US.

Outside of town, however, it's a long drive through the vast stretches of pine and spruce and birch trees to other population centers. That explains why McMurray Gospel Assembly's youth group ended up chartering a coach bus a few years back to go to a winter weekend retreat at a sister church in Fort Saint John, British Columbia—*eleven hours* away. They would roll out well before sunrise on a Friday morning, arrive in time for the evening kickoff, have Saturday meetings, stay through the host church's two Sunday morning services, and then begin the long trek back east again, not getting home until around midnight.

Paul Vallee, the youth pastor at the time, had worked hard to sign up forty-some young people for the trip, plus half a dozen adults. However, he couldn't quite convince one sixteen-year-old named Kelsey.[1] "I really wish I could go," she said wistfully, "but every time I take a long trip, it seems I get one of my migraine headaches. And once they start, they just kill me for three days or even four. I can't risk it."

The youth pastor thought about the fact that she had gone forward in the church more than once to be anointed with oil and prayed for. Still, her pounding pain and nausea kept coming back. Now he could only say to the girl, "Well, we'll just have to trust God about that."

Her girlfriends did some arm-twisting about the retreat, to the point that she finally caved in to their pleading. She happily boarded the bus that early morning with the rest.

However, about an hour and a half down Provincial Highway 63, sure enough … someone came up the aisle to where Paul and his wife, Patty, were sitting in the front row. "Kelsey's having problems," the person said. Paul went back to find the girl in excruciating pain. Her eyes had rolled back in their sockets as she gripped her head with both hands. She softly moaned. Concerned teens on all sides leaned up on their knees to see what was unfolding.

Now what? Pastor Paul knew they were still more than an hour from the nearest gas station where her parents could be called (in this pre-cell phone era) to come pick her up. Her suffering was intensifying by the minute. There had to be a better solution.

"Listen up, everybody," he said suddenly. "She told me this might happen. But we're going to pray. We're going to believe God for a miracle." He then began to lead out in prayer, with the teenagers joining in fervent pleas for divine intervention. From

34

the front to the back, the chorus swelled: "Oh, God, help Kelsey! Please stop this terrible headache! We believe you can do this." For the next twenty minutes, the bus became a rolling prayer meeting.

In time, the girl's body seemed to relax slightly from its earlier tension. She slumped back into her seat as the voices subsided, although kids kept praying quietly around her. Paul returned to his seat up front.

It was not long afterward when there was a tap on his shoulder. He looked up, surprised to see Kelsey herself with a calm demeanor. "This is a miracle, Pastor Paul," she uttered. "This has never happened in my life!"

She went on to explain: "Once these migraines start, they run their course. But … but … I'm better!" The entire bus broke out in rejoicing and thanks.

Ripple Effect

The Fort McMurray group had much to celebrate when they arrived at the retreat site. Paul Vallee spoke that Friday night on the baptism in the Holy Spirit. God's presence seemed especially strong in the meeting. "I was done speaking by eight thirty or nine," he remembers, "but kids were still at the altar at eleven thirty, being filled with the Spirit, speaking in tongues, awash in the flow of God. Some said, 'I don't even know what's happening to me'—though I thought I'd done a good job of explaining in my message! It was pretty dramatic.

"The Holy Spirit's move was so strong throughout the weekend that when we got back onto the bus Sunday afternoon to start home, kids were still weeping as we drove. They came home and began starting their days on their knees before the Lord. Parents said to me, 'What's happened to my kid? I go by his room in the early morning and see a light under the door. If I knock and he says, "Come in," he's there with his Bible open, and he's praying!'"

Some youth group members began voluntarily tossing out unhealthy media they'd collected, without any sermons on the subject. The Holy Spirit was doing his own deep, internal work in their hearts.

Soon, the senior pastor asked if some of the teens might want to share their recent experience with a Sunday night audience of adults. Paul Vallee thought they might be intimidated—but when he put the question to the group, a total of thirty-two hands went up. It turned out to be one of the most memorable services the church had ever experienced.

Kelsey and her family ended up moving back east to Newfoundland but stayed in touch with their Fort McMurray friends. Several years later, her update came through: "Since that day on the bus, I've never had a single migraine." God had done a permanent miracle in her body.

"Did We Kill Her?!"

In the small Ozark town of Ash Grove, Missouri (population 1,400), a sixtyish, dark-haired woman named Rue Duval stood out. Her strong Boston accent and French-sounding name told you she wasn't from around these parts. But she and her husband had retired here to be near a sister of hers, and the teenagers at the Assembly of God church had come to love her as a substitute grandma.

They were disappointed whenever they didn't see her on Sundays, which seemed to occur more frequently throughout one winter and spring. When they did see her, the short little woman, who had always smiled and given free hugs, wasn't quite her buoyant self. What they didn't know—and she didn't want them to know—was that she was undergoing radiation for a cancer that had now reached Stage 3.

"How I dreaded chemotherapy," she admitted later. "When the port was put in, I cried and hid from everyone the entire day."

The more the chemo took its toll, the harder it was to keep her secret. She finally confided in a close friend, who chided her for not letting others lift her up in prayer. Soon afterward, the pastoral staff and a few other adults were informed. They began to pray in earnest for Rue, of course.

But the steady decline continued.

Finally came a Wednesday night in May when, as the youth service was already underway in the main sanctuary, she silently stepped in at the back. Wearing her usual Christian-themed T-shirt and jeans, she took a seat on an usher's chair against the back wall. She could have gone to one of the adult Bible studies in other rooms of the church, but for some reason, she wanted to be close to "her kids."

As the worship music continued, Youth Pastor Amanda Starks glanced back and noticed her. "In that moment," she recalls, "I felt the Holy Spirit say, *You need to pray for her.* But I didn't know how she would feel about that. Would she want the kids to know she had cancer? They would be upset."

While another song proceeded, Amanda left the front to walk back and quietly say to the woman, "Rue, I really feel as if the Holy Spirit wants me to pray for you—but not just me by myself. He wants the kids to pray for you. Would you be okay with that?"

"Yes," she quietly replied. The youth pastor smiled and gave her a pat on the shoulder, then returned to the front to await the conclusion of the worship time.

She knew she would need to set up the prayer event carefully, especially since this group of sixty or so kids included a wide mix of backgrounds. Many came from unchurched and even troubled homes, having ridden one of the church buses to come alone on Wednesday nights. They didn't know much about church traditions.

"I'm glad to see that Rue stopped by tonight," she began,

which prompted young heads to swivel around toward the back. "We all love her; she's part of our 'family' here. But she's dealing with some tough physical stuff these days.

"I don't want you to be alarmed—but I will go ahead and tell you that she has been diagnosed with cancer. The chemo isn't working. She needs a miracle."

Some of the students caught their breath at this announcement. This was the woman who had taken them to Sunday lunches or helped pay their fees to go to camp. Pastor Amanda plunged ahead. "I feel like God wants to heal her tonight. And he wants to do that through you guys, as you pray for her.

"So here's what we're going to do: I'm going to ask Rue to come forward here to the altar area, and let's all just surround her as we pray. The closest ones can put a hand on her shoulder, and the rest of you can touch the person in front of you."

Some kids in the group remembered praying previously for a cheerleader's sprained knee, and had seen the girl pull off her brace on the spot, leaving it on the altar. But this was cancer!

Amanda, at the edge of the cluster with a microphone, began to lead out: "Lord, we believe that you are the Great Healer, and nothing is too hard for you. We're praying tonight for our friend Rue. We speak life to her body. I curse the very root of cancer, right down to the cell level ..." The teenagers joined vocally in their own words, beseeching God to intervene, while she closed her eyes and lifted her hands.

Suddenly—Rue's knees buckled, and she fell to the floor, overcome by the Spirit's power. Nobody pushed her; she collapsed all by herself, without warning.

"The kids' expressions at that moment were priceless!" Pastor Amanda remembers. "They were like, 'Oh, no! What did we do? We killed Rue!'"

Their youth leader didn't react but kept leading the prayer

expressions. The worship team began singing the song "Healing Is Here." Some of the words say:

> Sickness can't stay any longer
> Your perfect love is casting out fear
> You are the God of all power
> And it is Your will that my life is healed[2]

The group sang that song over and over while Rue lay on the carpet for at least twenty minutes. Somehow she ended up with her head under the front pew. Eventually she rolled sideways and sat up, laughing. Immediately she said to everyone, "I've been healed! I know it. I don't have any pain anywhere—not even in my knee, which has arthritis. Praise the Lord!" This brought a loud cheer and clapping from the teenagers.

Fully Convinced

She never wavered in her claim. The very next day, she was regaling townspeople at the post office and the grocery store with the story of what God had done for her through the youth group. Word spread quickly through the small community.

A week later, when the next chemo treatment was due, Rue Duval returned to her doctor, confidently telling him the same account. "Take this port out—the cancer is gone," she insisted. "I don't need chemo anymore."

"Well, that remains to be seen," the doctor said. "We'll need to do some blood work, to make sure you're okay."

"I *know* I'm okay," she interrupted. "Take it out!"

The doctor could hardly refuse a patient's clear directive, so he removed the device. But he also took blood samples and sent them to a lab for analysis. They came back clean.

That freed Pastor Amanda to endorse this as a genuine, verified healing to her teens. She also took time to explain the reaction they had seen during the prayer time. "If I were to go stick my finger in a light socket," she said, "I would feel a jolt of electricity through my body. I'd jump back. If it were powerful enough, I might even fall over.

"The power of God can be like that, only greater. When you encounter that power, your body can sometimes fall backward. It's very understandable, once you think about it."

Three weeks later, Rue's doctor prescribed a secondary PET scan. After that, she was declared cancer-free. She remains healthy to this day, helping other people, loving teenagers, and living a full and active life.

The whole episode has strengthened the teenagers' faith. "They don't really ask if God heals; they assume God is going to heal," says Pastor Amanda. "They have no doubt."

When fresh needs for healing arise, the students are the first ones to jump in. One Sunday morning, a woman came forward with a completely torn rotator cuff in her shoulder. Young people and others prayed confidently for her restoration. Her doctor later confirmed that the cuff and labrum were whole once again.

The entire church—youth and adults alike—have been brought to the next level of faith in a God who hears, who cares, and who heals. Teenagers grasp this truth as fast as anyone.

To watch a TV version of this account, go to: http://www1 .cbn.com/content/grandmother-healed-youth-service.

chapter 7

THE LUNCH
THAT MULTIPLIED

W elcome, everyone, to Calvary Temple!" the eager young
pastor said that Sunday morning back in early 1968. "As
you can tell, our church is new in this community, and we want to
get to know as many of you as possible.

"In fact, next Sunday after the service, we're going to have a potluck lunch downstairs. If you'd like to know more about us and what
we hope to accomplish here in Naperville, please come join us!"

Looking over the three or four dozen faces in the audience
that day, Bob and Karen Schmidgall could only hope and pray
that God would bless their efforts here in this western suburb of
Chicago. They were thankful that the Illinois District Assemblies
of God had managed to acquire this small white church building
on a side street that another denomination was selling. It wasn't
fancy or impressive by any means, but it had a modest parsonage
next door, where the pastoral couple lived, along with a young
intern who had come to help them temporarily.

On the following Saturday, Karen prepared her dish to share:
a package of noodles and a pound of hamburger that would

combine, when reheated on Sunday, to make a cheap version of stroganoff. She made sure there would be enough paper plates, napkins, and plastic utensils for the group, along with paper cups for water and coffee.

The morning service ended, and people began descending the steps to the church basement for the meal. Pastor Bob warmly welcomed moms and dads, some with their children, older couples, some singles—a goodly turnout ... while his wife couldn't help noticing that no one was carrying any food! They had certainly heard the word *lunch* in the announcement but apparently missed (or failed to understand) the word *potluck*. Karen glanced at her small bowl of noodles and her equally small bowl of hamburger topping and began to panic.

She quickly ran next door to grab a quart of green beans she had canned the previous summer, a quart of homemade apple sauce, and a loaf of bread. This would not come close to satisfying the appetites gathering in the room, but what else could she do?

The blessing for the meal that day may have sounded routine, but to at least the pastor's wife it was a desperate cry for help. As the first guests began to fill their plates, Karen quietly whispered to her handsome, six-foot-three husband, "Don't eat! And I won't, either. We don't have enough for everybody. I hope they don't take very much."

Bob Schmidgall, still basking in how many people had shown up, replied blithely, "Oh, don't worry about it. It'll be okay."

Karen thought to herself in that moment, *Well, you may not be worried about it, but I sure am! This is going to get really embarrassing.*

"Go ahead and start your talk about the church," she instructed her husband. "Maybe they'll be distracted from the lack of food." With that, she dashed out the door for a second rummage of her tiny kitchen, looking for anything else she could bring without having to cook it first—this time, no such luck.

By the time she returned, she found to her amazement that everyone was busy eating—and her two serving bowls were still half full. Had people held back and taken small portions? No, not really. Even her husband now had a plate! Karen stood motionless in shock.

"Hey, everyone," his booming voice rang out, "there's still food left. Come on back for seconds!" Chairs scraped against the concrete floor as people rose to get in line a second time, while Karen could only sink down into a chair, speechless.

Mysterious Abundance

When the meeting finished that afternoon, the Schmidgalls began cleaning up. To Karen's amazement, the serving table *still* had leftovers—enough to pack up an additional meal for the coming week.

"Do you realize what happened here, Bob?" she said to her husband. "I brought enough stroganoff for maybe six people!" He could only shake his head in amazement.

In years to come, Bob and Karen seldom spoke to others about the multiplying lunch. He never mentioned it from the pulpit. But the little church on the side street steadily grew under the gracious provision of God, to the point that today it draws 7,000 worshipers a week to a 120-acre campus on a major highway. Bob Schmidgall passed away suddenly the week of his fifty-fifth birthday (1998), but his confidence in a miracle-working God had laid a solid foundation.

"We didn't want to sensationalize anything," says Karen, who lives today outside Washington, DC. "God helped us that early Sunday because this was his work, not ours. His gifts aren't meant to make people say, 'Oh, wow—look at that special person,' but rather to meet a real and present need. That's the kind of God he is."

THE LONG
TUG-OF-WAR

The saints at Timmons Temple Church of God in Christ[1] (Springfield, Missouri) had set aside two weeks for a special "prayer revival." No guest speaker had been invited; instead, they determined to fast during the day and then gather at the church Monday through Friday evening from seven to eight o'clock for nothing but prayer. On the final Friday night, they would pray all through the night until six the next morning.

"We wanted all of God's presence and power we could receive," says the pastor at that time (now Bishop Elijah H. Hankerson III). "But on one of the final nights, we got a 'visitation' we weren't expecting."

A faithful young woman in the church had brought her mother-in-law, Molly,[2] to the service. The woman had been a devout Christian growing up in Oklahoma, but the racial prejudices of that era had embittered her. Adding insult to injury, her husband had abandoned her and said he didn't love her. In response, she had turned to black magic as a way to retaliate. She relished putting curses on others.

Now in her fifties, she wanted to be reclaimed by the Lord, said the daughter-in-law.

So Pastor Hankerson asked the woman to come to the altar. At first she seemed to welcome the prayers over her, loudly exclaiming, "Yes, Lord! Yes, Lord!"

But within two minutes, her sounds turned into growling. Her eyes glazed over, she fell to the floor, and a male voice from deep within her barked, "No! You can't have her. We've taken her!"

The people all around were taken aback. What was this? Hankerson explains, "This was back in the 1990s, and at that early point in my ministry, I didn't yet have much experience dealing with demon possession. I began dialoguing with the demon, which wasn't the smartest thing to do. 'Where have you taken her?' I foolishly asked."

"We have her now, and you can't take her," came the reply.

"Where did you take her?" the pastor asked again.

"We're not going to tell you!"

Earnest prayer for the woman's deliverance resumed. The group pled with God to step into this awkward situation and help this poor soul. Time went on, and their battle seemed to be stalemated.

At one point, the demon complained, "You're hurting her! You're hurting her!" But the believers would not be dissuaded, even as the night grew late.

Then … everyone sensed a new oppressive presence of evil in the building. The demon, which had been insisting, "I'm not coming out!" now changed to say, "I *can't* come out!"

"Why not?" the pastor wanted to know.

"Because he's gonna get me!"

"Who is that? Who's going to get you?"

"He's gonna get me—don't you see him?" the demon replied. "He's right behind you, all big and ugly!"

The pastor and prayer warriors looked around and saw nothing. But they *felt* something ominous in the sanctuary. They began to plead ever more urgently for the protection of the blood of Jesus.

"And then," the pastor recalls, "we could literally sense something retreating down the center aisle and out the door. We never did *see* anything, but we knew for sure that the superior Enemy had been expelled."

The resident demon still kept taunting the believers. Again, someone said, "What's your name?"

The demon said nothing. But in that instant, the woman opened her eyes, regained her composure, and answered in a normal female voice, "My name is Molly—what am I doing down here on the floor?"

Great rejoicing and laughter broke out. She smiled as she looked around at the group. The pastor said, "Don't you know what just happened?"

"No. What's going on?" She had no idea what had transpired since she had started toward the altar three hours previous.

Before the night was finished, Molly had been led to repent of her sins, to renounce all connections to the demonic world, and to accept Jesus Christ as her Lord and Master. Furthermore, within fifteen minutes, she was filled with the Holy Spirit and speaking in tongues.

She was soon baptized in water and went on to become an earnest church worker. In later years, she was licensed as an evangelist-missionary in the Church of God in Christ. The one who had served the dark powers for several decades became a shining light of truth and freedom, affecting many others in search of God's peace.

chapter 9

ON THE EDGE
OF DISASTER

The Sunday morning service at Believers Church in Douglasville, Georgia, just west of Atlanta, was coming to an end. Pastor Gene Evans had finished his message and was moving toward a call for response, when suddenly he paused.

"I don't usually do this kind of thing," he said in a steady voice, "but the Lord has given me a word just now that somebody here is planning to commit suicide. God wants you to know he has something better for you. Don't do what you're thinking of doing; let God be in charge of your life."

The congregation of two hundred or so didn't openly react, even though their minds were no doubt abuzz. As people were leaving that day, a middle-aged man approached the pastor. Jim Webb, husband and father of two young adults, was, in fact, the church's praise-and-worship leader. "That word was for me," he quietly revealed. "Things have been going really badly in my business, to the point I've been ready to just give it all up." The two men prayed together for the Lord to help stabilize his situation, then shared a big hug.

The backstory was that this man, a successful commercial artist and photographer, who had served as an art director at Six Flags Atlanta before opening his own business creating large scenics for theme parks and other clients, had hit rough waters. A partnership with his half-brother to provide the construction aspects had soured, forcing Jim to start over with a separate company. He ended up pouring so much personal savings into the venture that he and his wife, Linda, lost their home and one of their cars as well. "I was just sinking into depression," he remembers. "I couldn't see how we could ever recover from this financial pit."

Now his plan for suicide was mapped out. He would have lunch with his wife, then go to his office on Sunday afternoon, as he often did to get things in order for his fifty employees on Monday morning. There in his desk, his loaded gun would be waiting. The goodbye note he had written was already placed where Linda would find it.

But after the word of knowledge in church this morning, he sat quietly at his desk. "I knew the Lord had stopped me just in time," he says. "I was broken—to think that God would speak a message to me in my darkest hour." Leaving the building, Jim drove to the nearby Chattahoochee River and flung the weapon into the water.

Back in his vehicle, he noticed his cell phone had for some reason been turned off. He restarted it—and suddenly, "It blew up with about twenty messages," he says. "Linda had found my note and was frantic, like, 'Where are you!!! Please please please call me!!!' She had called Pastor Evans, so he was trying to reach me too." Within minutes, Jim was pulling back into his driveway safe and sound, to the relief of everyone.

In the months that followed, the new business kept struggling and eventually had to be closed, especially when orders almost dried up following the shock of 9/11. But through it all, the Lord made a way for this couple. Today, nearly two decades later, they keep trusting God as their supplier while they live in semi-retirement back in Florida. Jim continues to do occasional art projects.

"I'm still humbled that the Lord cared about me enough to intervene," he says, "and that the pastor obeyed in giving out that word in the church. I wouldn't be here today if he hadn't. It just goes to show that when the Spirit nudges you to use one of his gifts, don't brush it off. A life may be depending on your obedience."

chapter 10

FAITH TO GIVE

What if the Holy Spirit nudged you to give away something truly essential to your daily life? Not just a trinket, a souvenir, or an extra bed or chair. Say, your main *vehicle*?

That is what Cathy Ciaramitaro tried to tell her husband, Rick, the senior pastor of Windsor (Ontario) Christian Fellowship one day, after praying about a family with six children in their congregation. Some of them were enrolled in a Christian school, which only added to the bills of a large household. Their van, perhaps fifteen years old, was breaking down repeatedly.

"I was praying that God would somehow provide for their needs," she says, "when I started to feel that God was saying in response, *Give them your van.* "

Her first thought was, *So then, what are WE going to drive?!* This pastoral couple had one married daughter but five more kids of their own still at home. Their Ford Aerostar van, less than two years old, was their main form of transportation. Yes, they also had an old sedan, which seated only five with any comfort. And their teenage children were getting taller by the month.

But the more Cathy prayed, the stronger the directive came into her head. "I felt a stirring, almost an excitement, on the inside," she remembers. She finally summoned the courage to mention it to her husband. The response was swift: "No, Cathy. Don't be ridiculous. We're not giving our van away."

"Well, why don't you at least pray about it?" she replied. He said he would.

After a week with no update, she broached the subject again. "What are you thinking now about giving those folks our van?"

His answer was as firmly negative as the first time.

"Well … did you pray about it?" she asked.

"No, not really," the pastor admitted.

"Please promise me that you'll pray about this, Rick," she pled. He agreed.

A Curious Plague

Within the next month, a flurry of mechanical problems broke loose with the Ford van and the older car: flat tires, an exhaust system that fell off, transmission noises, battery problems, plus a break-in by a thief. It was uncanny. The straw that broke the camel's back was when smoke started pouring out of the van's steering wheel as Rick was driving downtown on an errand. He darted into the nearest service station and yelled, "I need a fire extinguisher!" (Only later, after the fire had been put out, did Rick learn that there'd been a manufacturer's recall for this hazard.)

Reviewing this odd convergence of problems, Rick couldn't help identifying with the Pharaoh in ancient Egypt who had kept resisting a divine message—only in this case, it was *Let my car go!* Every time he had told his wife no, something else had gone wrong.

Now, he finally surrendered. "Okay," he said to Cathy, "we'll get this steering wheel fixed, and then we can give the van away. We don't have the money to buy another one, so we'll just have to get along with the old car for a while. But, I agree with you: God is trying to tell us something here."

United in faith at last, the couple broke the news to their children around the dinner table. The younger generation was hardly impressed; groans and eye-rolling broke out. "So how are we all going to get around?" they wanted to know. The seven-teen-year-old son said, "Dad, this is the stupidest thing you and Mom have ever done."

Rick could only reply, "Well, God is going to provide for us— and when he does, you're going to eat those words."

Transfer Day

When the church couple was called and told they'd be getting a late-model van, they were naturally overjoyed. "Are you sure you want to do this?" they asked.

"Yes, we really believe God has told us to do this," Rick replied. "I have a couple of things to do to get it all cleaned up for you, and then let's meet next Monday at the ServiceOntario bureau to transfer the title."

After the paperwork was completed that day and the keys handed over, the couple and Rick walked outside. There was an awkward pause. Finally, the man said, "Is someone coming to pick you up?"

"No," the pastor answered. "Actually, could you drop me off at the church office?" They said yes, of course. En route, however, they asked several times if this transfer was something that really should be happening. "Yes," Rick replied. "We have no doubt that God wants us to do this. So, you just take the van and be blessed!"

Odd Call

Tuesday passed without incident, other than scrambling to get all seven family members where they needed to go. Nothing was said among congregation members about the gift. People who noticed the absence of the pastor's van just assumed it was back in the shop getting fixed after another breakdown.

On Wednesday morning, Cathy—feeling a bit anxious by now, since this whole thing had started with her—went to the church sanctuary to pray by herself. *God, I really believe you're going to provide,* she said. *I don't care what you provide. We just need another vehicle, new or old. Please do something!*

In the silence, an impression came into her mind: *Go into the office. Your answer is there.*

Cathy rose from her knees and walked to the office. "Oh, Cathy," the receptionist said, looking up. "So-and-so called and wants to meet with you and Pastor Rick. He said it would take only a few minutes. Here's his phone number." The name on the paper was that of a man in his late forties who was general manager of an industrial company, owned by one of the church's leaders. He had been attending for only a month or two, so the pastoral couple didn't know much about him yet.

Cathy hesitated, because with a midweek service coming up that evening, her husband was secluded in his office preparing his message and was not to be disturbed. She went ahead, however, to open the door and speak to Rick. "Somehow, I have the feeling that this might relate to God answering our need," she said.

When they called the man, he asked if he could come over right away. Without explaining his intent, he said he would take just five or ten minutes. Soon he arrived.

Sitting down in the office, he began, "During last week, I started feeling as if God was telling me to buy you a vehicle. I wrestled with that idea all weekend. I wasn't sure … so then on Monday, I mentioned it to my boss (the owner of the company). He listened to me and then said, 'If you want to do this, I'm in.'

"So, I'm here today to tell you that he and I believe God has told us to purchase you a new vehicle—any kind you want!"

Rick's and Cathy's jaws dropped. The very day, Monday, that they had quietly given away their van without telling anyone, the two men were agreeing to replace it with something brand-new.

"Well," the pastor finally replied after catching his breath, "with the size of our family, I guess we'd be interested in another van."

"That's fine," the man replied. "Any particular kind?"

Rick expressed his desire for one of the Chrysler models. Again the man spoke up. "Fine—I know the owner of the Chrysler dealership here. I'll call him right now. You guys can go down there and pick out the one you want—and it will be paid for."

That afternoon, the somewhat dazed couple went shopping at the car dealership, intending to choose a basic model. The owner was waiting to meet them. "No," he said, motioning with his hand, "here are three vehicles you can consider. Each of them carries the extended warranty. See which one you'd like." All three were fully equipped, top-of-the-line models. Within an hour, Rick and Cathy were driving home, shaking their heads at God's provision.

Surprise!

Their children, as one might imagine, were blown away that evening. The son who had made the earlier "stupid" crack took one look out the window and said, "Nice van in the driveway, Dad. Whose is it?"

"It's ours," his father replied.

"I thought you said you weren't going to buy another car!"

"Well, it's a blessing from the Lord," Rick explained, and went on to tell the details of what had transpired. Soon, everyone was outside exploring the bells and whistles the new van had to offer. The son was especially impressed to discover air-conditioning vents in the back where he usually sat, a feature the Ford Aerostar had lacked.

"This divine miracle of provision made a great impact on all our children," Cathy says today. "They've all grown up to evidence a spirit of generosity; they love to give and help other people. Eight of our married children and spouses are working with us in various ministries at the church, in fact.

"They have learned, as my husband likes to say, that 'the seed that leaves our hands never leaves our lives.' God has better things in store for his people than we can even imagine. As we listen to his voice and exercise the gift of faith, there's no predicting what will unfold."

chapter 11

DOOMED IN THE WOMB

Pregnancy can be one of the greatest seasons as a couple looks forward to the coming of their precious baby. And if two babies are on the way, the joy is doubled.

But not if something goes wrong. A Houston woman named Evangelina Garza explains.

I was excited at the news I would have twins. But fourteen weeks into the pregnancy, my doctor performed an ultrasound and confronted me with shattering news. The twins, both boys, were suffering from a complication called "twin-to-twin transfusion." The doctor explained that the blood of one twin, Elijah, was passing through to the second, Nehemiah. Elijah was retaining no blood for himself. Consequently, he was literally starving to death.

In a short space of time, this lack of blood supply had caused his tiny body to become stuck to one side of the uterus. He was "shriveling up like a raisin," the doctor said. If this continued, the prognosis would be bleak.

Elijah was gaining barely an ounce of weight each month. At this stage of development he had, we were told, at best a 50 percent chance of survival and a grim 75 percent certainty of mental retardation. Test results, which included a sonogram, confirmed this prognosis.

Nehemiah, on the other hand, had complications because he was receiving *too much* blood. His tiny heart was oversized and working extremely hard as it struggled to circulate the expanded supply of blood. The doctor diagnosed him with cardiomegaly (an enlarged heart). His heart valves were not closing properly, which allowed blood to flow back into the heart chamber. The heart had no rest; we were told his heart could give out at any time.

Our doctor sent my husband, Isaias, and me to see a heart specialist at Texas Children's Hospital in the world-famous Houston Medical Center. It was very rare for a woman to have an echocardiogram while carrying a baby in utero, but the doctor wanted us to see for ourselves how sick Nehemiah truly was. Nehemiah's heart was not circulating blood properly. It had leakage and backflow. He was, the cardiologist said, the sickest baby in utero he had ever seen in his life.

In an effort to become as educated as possible and give my babies every chance to live, I agreed to every test the doctors ordered. I saw the bleak results of each test with my own eyes. I spent countless hours grieving and praying over the young lives inside of me. There was no explaining why this was happening; I could only cry out to God to help us, to make right anything and everything that had gone so tragically wrong. I asked God not to let my dear unborn sons suffer for something that was beyond their control.

In times like this it is very easy to play the blame game and take on false responsibility. The Enemy screams in your ear, *Where is your God now?* Maintaining faith and subduing doubt and fear in complex times is the key to victory, but this is very difficult to do when every word you hear is negative.

"Zero Chance"

Because Nehemiah's blood flow continued backing up, his heart failed. His body and brain were not getting an ample blood supply despite receiving all of Elijah's blood. Because of this, his organs began to collapse and shut down.

By the twentieth week, Nehemiah began to bloat as if his body had begun the process of decomposition. We were told Nehemiah's brain was 95 percent damaged; he was now given "0 percent" chance of surviving.

In the face of such dire news, I was a basket base. Emotionally, I felt I could not go on; mentally, I was completely spent.

The picture being painted for me was absolutely horrifying. Nehemiah had three centimeters of fluid surrounding his brain, causing his face to look deformed. His scalp could not close at his fontanel (known as the "soft spot") because of excess fluid.

When we reached this point, the pressure increased for us to terminate the pregnancy. Our doctor wanted us to have a 3-D ultrasound to show us our twins were not normal-looking and would be born grotesque if the pregnancy continued. He said both boys should be taken at twenty-two weeks. Because this type of ultrasound could not be carried out in the medical center, I would have to fly to Florida for this procedure.

I was determined to give my unborn boys every possible chance for survival. I must confess that I did not dispute what the doctor was seeing. The regular ultrasounds were very revealing, even convincing. I cannot begin to describe my heartbreak as I saw the images again and again, revealing the complications with my unborn twins.

My husband, Isaias, was grasping for hope just as I was. He told the doctor we needed time to decide what we were going to do, knowing the decisions that were to be made would literally be a matter of life and death.

"Time?" the doctor said, obviously upset. "What more proof do you need? I can guarantee you these twins have *no life in them anymore*; it's time to make a decision and let them go."

He wasn't far off the mark. The doctor said that if Elijah

passed, Nehemiah would soon follow. As long as Elijah lived, even though he weighed only a few ounces, Nehemiah had a chance of survival. If Nehemiah died, Elijah would have a chance because he would then keep the blood supply that was flowing through to his twin.

The situation was beyond complicated; it seemed the worst situation any parents could possibly face.

In an act of desperation, the doctor recommended we help Elijah by clamping off Nehemiah's umbilical cord. In my mind, this would be an act of total desperation. Clamping the umbilical cord would stop all oxygen and blood to Nehemiah. He would most certainly die, and I would carry one living and one dead fetus until my delivery date. As far as I was concerned, I had not yet heard what I believed to be a viable option.

We were pressed to make the hardest decision of our lives. I cannot begin to describe the anguish we experienced. No matter what we did or decided, one of our boys would more than likely die, and the other would be born deformed and confronted with health challenges that would not only alter our lives, but also his from birth to death.

The doctor gave us a week to decide. A week is hardly time to decide on purchasing a home, let alone the future of two unborn children. We prayed earnestly and continually, but nothing seemed to be improving. Life seemed to go both in slow motion and fast-forward all at the same time. Every tick of the clock amplified the words of the doctor: "It is time to make a decision and let them go."

Nehemiah's heart was now the size of his chest, and because of amniotic fluid around his heart, abdomen, and lungs, his bladder and kidneys began failing. We knew his life was becoming more fragile by the moment. Our decision loomed before us like a huge funnel cloud from which there was no shelter for protection. We were told very emphatically that he had only one week to live.

Showdown

The week passed, and remarkably, Nehemiah was still alive. His breathing was not labored, and his movements were normal. The doctor couldn't understand it.

"For sure, Nehemiah is a fighter," he said, "but this baby will be dead in three days or less, *no more.*"

We realized the doctors were doing the best they could, delivering a prognosis based on what their education, equipment, and medical science were telling them. But, we knew we served a God who could do the impossible.

"I've done all I can do," the doctor said. "If you don't go to Florida, I can't see you anymore. The risk to you in continuing this pregnancy is too high and complicated."

That is when faith took hold of my husband. He grabbed me by the hand and pulled me up from the ultrasound table. "Let's go!" he said.

"What are you doing?" said the doctor. "Where are you going?"

"Thank you, Doctor," Isaias said, "but we are not killing our babies. If God wants them to die, he will have to do it himself."

The doctor said, "If you think your twins will make it, then you're wrong. It will take a miracle for them to survive, and I've never seen a miracle in my entire medical career."

Isaias squared his shoulders. "Doctor, we might lose our boys, but we still trust in the Lord. Our God performs miracles!" We walked out the door as the doctor stared in disbelief.

Once outside, I began sobbing. I wanted to fall to my knees. I felt completely helpless and spent. It appeared to me that we were losing the fight, and I had no answers. I didn't know where to turn or what to do next.

In retrospect, I realize that when we come to the end of ourselves, God can do his best work. He intervenes in a way so no one else can take the credit!

All I could do was pull myself together, accept our decision to "walk things out," and let God decide who was to live and who was to die.

I cried out, *What do you want from us, Lord? What can I do? I'm in need of you and your healing hands. Please don't turn your back on us.*

I shouted at heaven, *Didn't you hear the doctor say that unless a miracle happens, they won't survive? Prove him wrong, Lord! Show him what you alone can do! Please don't let us down.*

We cried the entire drive home, praying in the Spirit and sobbing out loud. I have never known such intense anguish in my life.

One Sunday Night

That very Sunday night our church, CT Church in Houston, was having a "miracle and healing service." We decided to attend and believe God for a miracle of epic proportions. The service began with compelling worship; then a faith-building message was spoken from the Word of God. The remainder of the service was devoted to an extended time of prayer for specific needs.

That night a dear friend, Kim, took my hands and prayed with me, agreeing in faith that God was going to bring both boys through this ordeal, and they would live and not die. We prayed that Elijah and Nehemiah would be perfectly whole, despite the overwhelming evidence to the contrary.

Kim told me to write the date on a piece of paper and carry it with me so I would remember the day God healed my twins. I cannot begin to describe what that prayer time did for my faith. The words Kim spoke over me were the first positive words I had received in weeks! I did, in fact, write the date down; the day was Sunday, November 2, 2003.

We went back to the doctor the following Wednesday. I was very nervous because I was not sure how the doctor would respond to us. However, he was pleasant and sympathetic, and he performed another ultrasound.

As he worked the instruments, he said, "Here goes Baby B [Nehemiah]." He looked around and said it again: "Here goes Baby B." Then a look of confusion crossed his face. "Unbelievable," he said. A few seconds later he said it again, but with more emotion: "Unbelievable!"

Nehemiah's heart had shrunk to its normal size. There was still evidence of fluid around his brain, but his organs were functioning and there was little sign of sickness. Praise God! The doctor seemed stunned. He looked completely flabbergasted. My eyes were brimming with tears, and I whispered, *God!*

From the evening of that "miracle and healing service," the twins improved every single day. I was admitted to the hospital at week twenty-nine and stayed until my delivery five weeks later.

Before delivery, our doctor attempted to prepare us for the worst by telling us Nehemiah would more than likely take a first breath and expire due to exhaustion from the sickness. He said Elijah possibly would live. He ordered the neonatal intensive care unit (NICU) team to stand by in the delivery room just in case.

On February 2, 2004, the babies were born. They cried like normal babies cry, and from the outset they began breathing on their own! We were ecstatic.

How Did *That* Happen?

As soon as the twins were delivered, the doctor asked a nurse to bring him a carton of milk and syringes. He placed my placenta on the surgery table and began injecting the vessels with milk to see which veins were clogged and how the sickness might have happened.

Isaias was videotaping the boys in the nursery when the doctor sent for him. He wanted Isaias to record him injecting the placenta.

We still have the video of the doctor showing us where the blood vessels from the two boys intersected, which allowed Elijah's blood to move into Nehemiah. Then he showed us where the vessels "clogged up," which returned the blood flow to normal for both boys.

"It's a miracle," he said. "These blood vessels clogged up on their own as if performed by laser surgery." He told us no doctor would ever see such a thing. He was very clear that there was "no sign pointing to how the sickness began, but there is evidence how it ended. We will never know what happened."

He may never know how it happened, but we know God performed his own supernatural surgery and healed our twins. When Doctor Jesus performs a surgery, he doesn't need an operating room, a surgeon's scalpel, anesthesia, or any other conventional thing. He just does his precise laser surgery with his word!

The doctor said Nehemiah would spend half his life having ultrasounds and echocardiograms in Texas Children's Hospital, but this prediction proved to be completely wrong.

I took Nehemiah to his first follow-up appointment on March 31, 2004. The report that came back showed his heart was completely normal; he had the heart of a normal baby! He had no more need of echocardiograms. Both boys are perfectly healthy.

From beginning to end, this miracle had the fingerprints of God on it. He is a God who hears and answers prayer![1]

Now, more than a dozen years later, the Garza twins are heading into their teenage years in good health. "They're both very athletic," reports the family's pastor, Don Nordin. "They have a younger sister now, and we see them all in church regularly. What God did back in 2004 has stood the test of time."

chapter 12

NORTHERN TEST

When Ron Thorley's young wife started going to church at the invitation of a friend, he wasn't upset. But, neither was he inclined to join her. He felt he'd done well enough in life so far without God or religion.

Now in his early thirties, he already owned and operated a car wash in the snowy Upper Peninsula city of Marquette, Michigan, plus a number of rental properties. Frieda, his attractive, well-spoken wife, had a good job as a newscaster at the local NBC television affiliate. Together they were enjoying the DINK lifestyle (double income, no kids).

Once Ron became aware that his wife had become a committed Christian, he asked her one day, "What's the name of that church you're going to?"

"Marquette Gospel Tabernacle,[1] over there on Presque Isle Avenue," Frieda answered. "Right across from the university." He had noticed the handsome brick building once or twice while driving the city's main north-south artery but had never given it a second thought.

"What kind of a church is it?" he then asked.

"I guess it's what they call 'Pentecostal.'"

A frown came across Ron's forehead. "Is that the kind of place where they do that speaking-in-tongues thing?" he wanted to know.

"Well, actually, I've heard that a few times in some services," she replied honestly.

That ended the conversation for the time being. But some weeks later, Ron was curious enough to investigate further. Frieda was working on a news story that Sunday morning, so he ventured out alone. On the way, he put God to something of a test: *Look, if this tongues thing is for real, let it happen today.*

Entering the sanctuary, he saw 150 or so worshipers gathered for the morning service. First came the singing of various songs, none of which he knew. This gradually morphed into an unscripted time of praise and worship, with a number of voices raised simultaneously, using their own words.

And then … an older woman beside Ron in the same row suddenly began to speak out in an unfamiliar language, loudly enough that everyone could hear. He instinctively glanced sideways; she didn't look like "the type" to make a spectacle of herself. Her eyes were closed as she continued speaking for maybe sixty or ninety seconds, after which the room was quiet. Ron wondered what would happen next.

Then someone across the way in a different section began to speak in English, giving a message of encouragement. The phrasing was unique, as if God was channeling some kind of communication—only nothing was written down; it was all happening impromptu. This speech went on about the same length of time as the first, after which the worshipers murmured their thanksgiving.

Pastor Louis Ondracek then came to the pulpit and said, "For those who might be wondering about what we just heard, let me briefly explain: These were two of what the Bible calls 'spiritual gifts'—God's way of saying something directly to us as a congregation. First came the message in an unknown tongue, then the interpretation in a language we could all understand. And we welcome this as part of our worship this morning.

"If anyone has follow-up questions, I'd be glad to explain further after the service."

Following the sermon and closing prayer that day, Ron drove home with much to think about. Apparently, God was real after all. God had even heard his challenge a few hours earlier and promptly responded to it. When he told Frieda about it that afternoon, she quietly smiled.

Onward

The young couple began attending church together. Occasionally, the pastor would preach about the need for salvation, explaining what it takes for any human being to be right with God. He would follow up this kind of message with a public invitation for people to come forward and pray to receive Christ as their Savior.

Ron never did respond publicly, even though he was listening carefully. Eventually, the pastor and his wife went to visit them in their home. In this informal setting, Ron said, "Hey, I want you to know that in one of the services, I asked Christ to come into my life."

The Thorleys quickly showed signs of growth in their new faith, not only on Sundays but also in the Wednesday night services. They began inviting other young couples to their home for Bible studies. In a relaxed and gracious way, they lived out their Christianity and expressed it authentically. Eventually, Frieda's father and mother—unchurched as well—came to the services and decided to follow Christ like their daughter and son-in-law.

When the next chance arose to be baptized in water, the young couple said, yes. The ceremony was held outdoors at the "hot pond" alongside the city's power plant, where clean, warm water was discharged into a receiving basin before flowing on into chilly Lake Superior. For years to come, the couple's walk with God held steady and kept maturing, an example to all who knew them.

All because a church was willing to welcome the twin gifts of tongues and interpretation—on a Sunday morning no less.

chapter 13

HARD CASE

It's one thing to ask God to heal a temporary illness: pneumonia, a sinus infection, or an inflamed stomach lining. It's quite another to tackle a locked-in-from-birth congenital disorder like cerebral palsy. When the infant brain has been damaged or malformed while still in the womb, it doesn't "get better" with time. The awkward muscle movements, garbled speech, flailing limbs, and lack of balance are said to be permanent.

But ... "Is anything too hard for the LORD?"[1]

In this interview, condensed from *Message of the Open Bible* magazine (March-April 2017 issue), a Missouri woman named Marlene Klepees gives her amazing answer to that question.

You had a rough go of it in the beginning. You weighed only two pounds at birth and showed signs of cerebral palsy right away. Then, when you were only a year old, you lost your parents in a motorcycle accident. You were raised by great-grandparents for a while, and then foster parents. Tell us how you ever became a Christian at age eleven.

I was invited to a Youth for Christ meeting, where they showed a Billy Graham film that helped me recognize my need for Christ.

Afterward a speaker asked if anyone wanted to accept the Lord into their heart, and I did. In that moment, it was obvious to me that the leaders weren't sure I knew what was happening. But I definitely did, and the Father knew what was going on. He came into my life that night, and it changed the value of my life on earth.

You shared that you thought cerebral palsy was God's "assignment" for you.

My theology was not accurate in those days. I hadn't assumed there was an active Enemy at all. I thought everything that happened was ultimately God's plan, so I thought he created me with cerebral palsy. I didn't even look at it as negative; I just thought he would use it somehow because he would identify himself in me through suffering.

But at age seventeen, I began to realize that some things in life might not be his will. I was living out in the country then, without anyone to talk to me about the Lord. I didn't think I would ever have a job, ever be married, or do any of the normal things. I was isolated.

This became one of the greatest learning seasons in my life. I realized that while "all things work together for good,"[2] not all things are *planned* by God. I figured out that there's an Enemy who comes "only to steal and kill and destroy,"[3] and that Jesus came to give life more abundantly.

That realization changed everything.

Meanwhile, doctors had tried everything they knew. They finally sent you to the renowned Mayo Clinic. Was this like the last hope for you?

Yeah. Even there, they couldn't get my seizure activity to slow down. The good part at Mayo was that they realized I was more self-aware than people had thought in Missouri. I knew what was happening around me. I could partially move my eyes and also my mouth.

But after three months on a rehab floor, they said I should just go back to Missouri to a total-care nursing home. I became angry. I thought, *I'm nineteen now, and this is how God is going to leave me?!* I began yelling at God.

In that moment, the Father kept telling me, *I love you, and I am going to take care of it.* (I heard the voice internally, almost audibly.) His presence seemed to hit my room.

He showed me a picture of myself outside, riding a bike on beautiful, green grass. He also showed me a church with red carpet and light-colored woodwork. Finally, he showed me the words "March 29" in bright, bold letters—a date that was three weeks away.

So you were ticked off at God—but he lovingly wrapped you in his arms and gave you a picture of what was going to take place. Was it a dream or a vision?

I would say it was a vision. It was not something I was used to. But I knew it was God. There was no question that his presence was in my room, and I was very used to his presence. I was used to having him come and hug me and bring peace to me.

I didn't know a lot of Bible verses—the one, for example, that says he wants us to prosper and be in health just as our soul prospers.[4] I didn't know that Jesus had gone to the cross and was brutally beaten so we could have healing. But this vision told me that he wanted me to be healed.

I imagined in my mind how the vision would come to pass. But none of the things I imagined happened. March 28 came, and I was still lying there in Rochester. My family had gone back home. There wasn't anyone to take me to a church, which I was expecting after the vision. I thought I had goofed up, that God's plan wasn't going to happen, and I started repenting.

In that moment, God's voice simply went, *Hush.* I became

quiet, so I could receive from him. And then he said, *In the morning, have the nurse get the Yellow Pages. I will give you the name of the church and the person who is to pray for you.*

The next day, when the nurse came in to prepare me for the day, I tried to say, "Yellow Pages," and kept pointing to the phone book. When she opened up to the church section, two lines seemed to jump off the page. She read them: "Open Bible Church" and "Scott Emerson," who was the pastor there. But then she left the room.

She came back around 12:30 p.m. and dialed the number. When the pastor answered, she put the receiver to my mouth. I tried to talk, but he didn't understand very much of what I was trying to say. The nurse told him my room number, and then the call was over. We just waited after that.

Later that afternoon, Pastor Scott showed up in my room. As I described the details of my vision, he said, "That's my church; that's the carpet; that's the inside of the church."

Before long he was saying, "Let's get you to church. We have service tonight, and we'll pray for you." He began to try to make arrangements, which proved to be difficult. The nurse—obviously a Christian—started making phone calls to get permission for me to go out. She even lined up someone to cover her shift in case she needed to drive me. Finally, they got authorization for the pastor to load me into his car.

So you arrived at church that Sunday evening after all. Scott read appropriate Scriptures and announced they were going to pray for you.

Yes. I remember him saying something like, "I've never prayed for someone like this before." But then he started praying that God would heal me "from the top of her head to the soles of her feet."

Soon he was asking me if, by faith, I wanted to try to stand. I nodded yes, even though at this point my knees were bent inward, my body shook continuously, and I couldn't swallow a lot of my saliva. So they stood me up.

Suddenly, I could feel the floor under my shoes! I took a few steps, with others holding onto me. Then, they let go of me. From that point, every step got better and better. We took a few laps around the room. Everyone was rejoicing with me.

Pastor Scott announced that we were going to sing. At that point, my eyes got really warm. I heard the Father say to take off my glasses. As I threw them off, I realized my vision had been healed too!

What happened at the end of that service? Did you go back to Mayo Clinic?

Scott Emerson tells: I had prepared a sermon, but what could I do after this? We'd already had church! So we took Marlene to an ice cream shop on the way back. Everyone ordered a sundae except her. She wanted a cone.

But then, she simply sat there playing with it. "I've never held one of these before," she said.

When we returned to the clinic, a charge nurse saw Marlene walk in under her own power—and literally dropped the telephone. She had been telling everyone that she was going to be healed, that she was going to ride a bicycle, but they hadn't taken her seriously. Now a group of professionals gathered around her. She told them what God had done that night.

One woman said, "I've seen it, but I refuse to believe it. We'll see what this is like in the morning." The rest, however, were rejoicing.

Marlene again: After Pastor Scott left, all the nurses and staff gathered in my room trying to see what all I could do. When my doctor heard the story, he asked if I would stay until Tuesday morning so they could run some tests.

The doctors also had a conference that day. When I walked into that conference room under my own power, everyone stood up and began applauding. They asked all kinds of questions.

One person said, "Tell us about your vision" (meaning my eyesight). But I thought they meant the vision God gave me, so I started telling my whole story of the past few weeks. No one was disrespectful. In fact, as the conference ended, one doctor actually stood up and said, "Praise the Lord!"

My doctor's written report says:

"You returned to the rehabilitation unit that evening walking, something you'd never done since your admission to the unit. And when I saw you back at the clinic some weeks later, you'd improved even more. You were able to walk perfectly normally, and your eyesight had improved so much that you did not need to wear spectacles. We were all thrilled with the outcome."

Marlene, this happened back in the early 1980s. You're still walking normally. God's work has apparently "stuck."

I am blessed. I now run a flower shop, so I'm busy. I also get to travel extensively. I get to see a lot of healings. It's my personal belief that the scars of Jesus cause our healing. "The chastisement of our peace was upon him; and with his stripes we are healed."[5]

I hardly go through a weekend service or a week without someone being healed of something chronic: autism, ALS, other things. It's about the merit of Jesus, not our merit.

That very first night when we left the ice cream shop, I happened to see someone else in a wheelchair—and I knew I didn't deserve healing more than anyone else. Healing is not a reward for anything. It is a gift that comes through the cross.

No longer am I intimidated by what disease someone has, how long they've had it, or the intensity of their problem, because healing is based on the merit of what Jesus did. Not everyone I pray for gets healed—but I know that healing is God's will, just as it's his will for everyone to be born again.

God uses healing as a manifestation on earth, so that we will recognize his authority and submit our lives to him. He uses sickness to display his glory.

"Freely you have received; freely give," Jesus said to his disciples as he sent them out to heal and preach.[6] Freely, means without restriction, without restraint. That's what healing is all about.

To watch a five-minute video of Marlene Klepees' miracle, go to: www1.cbn.com/content/woman-healed-cerebral -palsy-through-vision.

chapter 14

CASTING OUT DARKNESS

Young San Diego pastor Loyd Naten was pleased, of course, to see a new family of four start to attend his church. The man worked as a heavy equipment mechanic while his wife was a full-time homemaker. Their son and daughter, both in elementary school, quickly plugged into Sunday school and children's church.

The pastor was mystified, however, by the woman's repeated prayer request when she would come week after week to the altar at the close of a service. He would ask, "What do you need the Lord to do for you, Cheryl?"[1] and she always gave the same generic reply: "Well, I just need God to touch my life." Without probing further, he laid a hand on her shoulder and prayed for the Lord's blessing upon her.

The next Sunday—same thing, over and over.

One Sunday evening, as she was making her way forward once again, the Lord spoke to him with a shocking revelation: *This woman is demon-possessed. She needs deliverance. But don't invite anybody else to join you as you pray for her. Handle this yourself.*

Says Pastor Naten, "I've never been one to attribute too much to the Devil; in fact, I don't think he can *possess* a truly born-again person. He can, however, *oppress* and harass them.

"But then, I didn't know Cheryl very well. Was she, in fact, even saved? Come to think of it, she always seemed to pick out a seat behind some taller person, so we couldn't see each other's eyes as I preached. Was she doing this on purpose? So many unknowns ..."

He came to pray for Cheryl once again that night and, almost without thinking, followed his usual pattern of welcoming others to help in interceding. They gathered around the woman and began calling on God to meet her need. She went down onto the floor as they summoned the power of the Lord to work in this case. The pastor laid his Bible on her midsection as a symbol of the almighty Word of God.

It became apparent that this was going to take a while. From time to time, she would raise her arms as if trying to sit up. Eventually, her voice began to shift in tone. "Take the Bible off!" she blurted out at one point. "I'm on fire!" she cried at another.

The prayer work, having started around seven p.m., continued for hours. The rest of the congregation gradually went to their cars, while the band of saints kept claiming victory over the Devil's grip until 11:30 p.m., by which time everyone was exhausted. "She never broke through to freedom," the pastor remembers, "and we were all disappointed. We finally gave up and headed home."

Rebuke

Before falling into bed that night, Pastor Naten was hit with a correction from the Lord: *I told you not to have anybody come pray with you. The reason was some of them might not believe she's actually demon-possessed. Tonight you had unbelief there in the circle praying with you. That's why she wasn't delivered.*

The pastor had no defense to raise.

A few days later, the couple came to his house, wanting to ask if she was actually demon-possessed. "Yes," the pastor replied.

They didn't try to dispute this conclusion. "Would you pray for us again?" they wanted to know.

Pastor Naten did so, but "I didn't feel anything happen that day," he remembers. This was proving to be a tougher challenge than he had expected.

Along the way, he learned that in her past she had indulged in a number of occult activities—watching demonic films and exploring the dark side. She had opened herself up to evil influences.

Another Try

Two weeks later, Cheryl was back in the evening service. Once again, she seemed to hide behind a larger person in the pew ahead of her. Nevertheless, she came again to the altar seeking help as the meeting concluded.

Immediately, the pastor heard God's voice in his mind, *Do you remember what I told you last time? Now,* you *pray for her.*

Loyd Naten was not about to make up his own strategy this round. He straightforwardly put his hand on her head and said, "I rebuke this foul spirit in the name of Jesus! I command it to come out of her."

Immediately, her countenance broke into a smile. She looked like a different person. Joy flooded her entire being. Hugging her husband, she exclaimed, "I feel so free!" Others gathered around to rejoice with her. It was obvious that Cheryl was at peace after being tormented for so long.

Before leaving the church that night, two members came to him and asked, "Pastor, did you see what happened when you prayed for that woman?"

"No. I just know she got deliverance."

"Well, when you prayed, we saw two green masses float out of her and head out the side door!"

"Really?! That must have been the demonic spirits."

Relapse

Unfortunately, this story does not have a happy ending. Cheryl did well for a couple of months, coming to church and following the Lord—but then dropped out of sight. The pastor tried repeatedly to call the home and could never get an answer.

Her sister-in-law reported later that on a Saturday night, Cheryl and her family had gone to see a new Hollywood movie about demons. They never darkened the church door again. It saddened him greatly.

"It reminded me of what Jesus said about an impure spirit being cast out of a person, but then wanting to return—with seven more companions. If successful, he said, 'the final condition of that person is worse than the first.'[2]

"I had talked with her and tried to counsel her, saying, 'Now there are some things you can't do. It's like, you can't pick up a smoldering stick and not get burned. You need to stay away from the things that got you into this bondage in the first place." Unfortunately, that advice wasn't followed.

Loyd Naten—who eventually rose to become general bishop of the Pentecostal Church of God—still insists that the name of Jesus is more powerful than any demonic force. "When we recognize what we're up against, we have the resource to take authority over it," he says. "Permanent deliverance is possible, provided we continue to walk in the light 'and do not give the devil a foothold.'"[3]

chapter 15

MAKEOVER IN THE MALL

From his home base in Vancouver, Jamie Rauch is a young evangelist with the Pentecostal Assemblies of Canada (PAOC) whose special calling is to influence people in the film and entertainment industry. He also leads churches on both sides of the border in "Lifestyle Evangelism" seminars, showing how to share the gospel freely and to pray for the sick wherever possible.

His training is more than just theoretical. In the wake of several sessions on understanding today's secular culture, responding to objections from unbelievers, demystifying fears, and bringing God's healing power into present needs, he sends everyone out to practice in teams. And that is how, in March 2017, he and two women attendees ended up on a Saturday afternoon in the large Everett Mall, north of Seattle.

"They'd never done this kind of thing before," he says, "but they were willing to step out in faith. So first, we went to Starbucks. The first woman struck up a fruitful conversation with a security guard. She found out she didn't need to be scared after all."

This emboldened the second woman to say that her daughter worked in a nearby cosmetics store. She wasn't on duty that particular day, but she had told her mother about a fellow employee named Mikayla[1] who used Lofstrand (forearm) crutches. The young woman, twenty-seven years old, managed to perch on a high stool and do makeovers, despite her chronic pain—a condition that had persisted ever since she was eight.

"Let's go there!" the mother said.

Before entering the store, Jamie led the others in a quiet prayer: "Lord, please give us favor and open the door so we can pray for this person." But when the trio entered and quickly spotted Mikayla, she was in the midst of working with a customer. Who knew how long this would last?

Within three minutes, however, she finished her makeover tasks. The mother approached her, introduced herself as her coworker's mom, and said, "I was just wondering … my friends and I would like an opportunity to pray for you. Would that be all right?"

"Well, I'm just now going on my break for fifteen minutes," Mikayla answered. "So, okay—why not? My parents are here to meet me on my break too. Can they come along?"

"Sure!"

While she was getting her jacket from the back room, the team met the parents and heard a little history. They found out the girl's hips were displaced and the surrounding cartilage and ligaments had long ago atrophied, resulting in bone-on-bone friction. Crutches had been the only way she could get around for nearly twenty years now. She had virtually no feeling in her legs or feet. The parents expressed how hard it had been watching their daughter grow up under such difficulty. Any sense of hope was minimal.

In a Matter of Minutes

Mikayla soon emerged, and the group of six formed a circle in the middle of the mall's busy concourse. While shoppers and their children passed by on either side, Jamie asked, "Are you in pain right now?"

"Oh, yes."

"How bad is it, on a scale of one to ten?"

"I'd say about a seven," she replied. "That's what I live with most of the time."

The two women from the church looked toward Jamie to lead the way at this point. He said, "Well, as we pray here today, is it okay if we put our hands on your shoulders?"

Mikayla said, "That's fine."

He then took a breath and declared, in a steady voice, "I now command the pain to go, in the name of Jesus. I command all feeling to come back into her legs. And I command there to be new hips now, in the name of Jesus." (In doing this, he illustrated a curious point from his teaching session, that *the longer you pray, the less faith you're showing.* "I tell people, 'Notice the way Jesus healed people. How much talking did he do? Very little—just "Get up!" or "Your sins are forgiven. Now you can go." We don't need to beg and plead for half an hour!'")

Now it was time for testing what had or had not happened to Mikayla. "Are you comfortable trying to walk down the hall here without your crutches?" he asked.

Having felt nothing unusual so far, she hesitated for a moment. Neither she nor her parents showed any sign of familiarity with God or his power to heal. But then she answered, "Uh, well, okay, I can try that." Handing her crutches to her parents, she began moving past a couple of stores unaided. She didn't stagger or flinch; her gait was steady. She then turned around and walked back to the group, a look of amazement on her face.

"I can feel my feet!" she exclaimed as she began lifting up her legs, first one and then the other.

"How's the pain?" Jamie inquired.

She thought for a minute, then said, "Not so bad now. Maybe a five."

Jamie replied, "Okay, then let's pray again," thinking that if Jesus prayed twice for the blind man outside Bethsaida,[2] mere mortals shouldn't hesitate to pray repeatedly. He then voiced the same short prayer he had said before. His reasoning: "If we've been given the authority of Christ, we can use that authority to tell the human body what to do."

Mikayla took a second trip down the concourse and back. Again, her walking was normal. This time, her pain was down to a three, she reported. She was speechless at what was going on in her long-compromised body. Her mother was crying by now, while her wide-eyed father stared into space, the color having drained from his face.

Eventually, she managed to comment, "My legs feel like they do the first thing in the morning, before I even get out of bed and try to go anywhere. That's the best part of my day. After that, everything gets worse and worse as the hours add up."

Jamie replied, "Okay, I'll pray just one more time, to see this healing become 100 percent." He repeated the same prayer as before, adding one extra sentence: "From the top of her head to the bottom of her feet, I command this body to be made whole, in the name of Jesus."

Mikayla went on yet another walk, this time raising her legs even higher, and twisting her pelvis to check for grinding, popping, or clicking. Nothing happened. Everything worked the way it was intended.

"I'm so confused! I don't know what's going on!" she exclaimed. "The pain is entirely gone this time!" The mother was absolutely bawling by now, while the father continued to look stunned. Mikayla began to cry as well.

Jesus' Love on Display

Eventually the jubilation calmed down to the point that Jamie and his teammates could put into practice what Jesus told the seventy-two who were sent out to minister: "When you enter a town and are welcomed … Heal the sick who are there and tell them, 'The kingdom of God has come near to you.'"[3]

In Mikayla's case, they said, "You know, Jesus loves you so much that he couldn't stand the fact that you've had limitations ever since you were eight years old. He wanted to make things right again for you.

"If you want to understand what just happened here, how about coming to Gateway Centre Church in Lynnwood tonight, where we'll be having a service? This will clear up a lot of your questions."

By now the fifteen-minute break was over, and Mikayla needed to get back to her cosmetics counter. "Thank you, thank you, thank you!" she bubbled as she hugged the three team members. She then pulled herself away to walk back into her store—leaving her crutches with her astounded mother.

Today, Jamie Rauch is not sure if Mikayla or her parents actually showed up that evening, or whether they had some kind of schedule conflict. He can say with assurance, however, that they will never forget the total makeover in the mall that restored her body far more than skin-deep. The love and power of Jesus had left its indelible impression for all time.

chapter 16

MODERN-DAY LAZARUS

Sometimes when a spiritual gift is needed, you don't even have time to think. A crisis erupts in front of you, and the Holy Spirit needs to take over.

Pastor Eric Angeles was getting organized for a Saturday morning board meeting at his home in metro Los Angeles when, out of the corner of his eye, he noticed a red pickup truck speeding down his residential street. It zoomed past his front window—but then a split second later, he heard an ominous thud. Brakes squealed, followed by more bumping sounds, as if something was rolling. *Must have hit a dog,* he thought to himself.

People began shouting in the street. "Go see what happened," the pastor called to his young-adult daughter, May. She opened the front door—and gasped to see not a dog, but a boy sprawled motionless on the pavement.

"Dad! Somebody's been hit! Call 9-1-1!"

While the call was underway, both May and the pastor's wife, Ruth, dashed outside to join the other neighbors and the distraught truck driver, who had come running back to the scene. A flurry of shouts in both English and Spanish filled the air. The boy appeared to be about eight or nine years old; his gaze was fixed;

his mouth gaped, but he made not a sound. His chest showed no sign of breathing. Various people looked for a pulse in his wrists, then his neck, and found none either place.

The Angeles family did not know him personally but realized the family lived in one of the houses across the street. Ruth joined a teenage girl and knelt down beside the boy. The pastor's wife did not know in that moment whether the boy was gone or not, but she knew what she could do.

"Would it be all right if I prayed for him?" she asked. The girl and her mother nodded.

Ruth began to intercede with all her might. "Lord, in the name of Jesus, bring back life into this boy! Perform a miracle right in front of our eyes! Death, you are rebuked from this scene!" The Spirit impressed Ruth to call out the boy's name, and when she asked for his name, the seventeen-year-old sister replied, "Leonel."

Then, like the Savior long ago in front of Lazarus' tomb, she began specifically calling out, "Leonel! Leonel! Come back, Leonel!"

The father was pacing back and forth, crying out, "He's dead! He's dead! My son is dead!"

Pastor Eric gently embraced him, saying quietly in his ear, "Don't panic; don't do anything rash just now. The Lord is in control." He could tell, however, that the man's English was not strong enough to absorb what he was saying. So in that moment, the Spirit gave a Spanish sentence to say: *¡Llame el nombre de Jesus!* ("Call on the name of Jesus!"). It had been a long time since the pastor (born in the Philippines) had studied Spanish back in college, so he certainly couldn't take credit for getting the conjugation correct. Now the sentence, fully formed, dropped into his mind and onto his tongue.

Upon hearing this, the father crumpled facedown onto the street, alongside the boy, joining the others who by this time were also already calling out the Lord's name, as he'd been instructed: *"Hay-SOOS! Hay-SOOS! Hay-SOOS!"* Urgent prayers continued to ascend all around. Even the truck driver was kneeling beside the boy and the others.

Around the fifth loud mention of Jesus' name, the boy took one big gulp of air. His eyes blinked once. He began to twitch.

"Hold him down," the pastor instructed. "Keep him still because he's probably broken some bones."

A few seconds later, the ambulance rolled onto the block with lights flashing. The EMTs jumped out with their equipment and began carefully examining him. They placed him on a stretcher and loaded him into the ambulance.

The emergency room X-ray and CT scans that day revealed a grave complex of injuries: a broken hip, several fractured ribs, a dislocated shoulder, a cracked collarbone, a skull fracture, blood clots in his head, and a spinal fracture. "He's conscious now," the doctor reported to the parents, "but it will take at least a month before he is strong enough to go home. I doubt he will be up and walking again before six months."

Aftermath

The day following the tragedy was a Sunday. Pastor Eric and Ruth left town after the evening service on a scheduled trip, not returning until Thursday evening. They had hardly set down their suitcases before there was a knock at their door. There stood the teenage sister who had translated for them at the accident scene. They now found out her name was Brianda.

"Could you come over to our house?" she said. "My mom wants to talk to you." The couple readily agreed.

When they walked into the family home—there was Leonel sitting upright and alert in a wheelchair! He wore a soft neck brace, and his left arm was in a sling to hold his shoulder in place.

But how had he gotten out of the hospital so soon? Yes, it is often said that children recover faster than adults, but to go from a month prediction down to just four or five days in the hospital seemed implausible. He sat there reading get-well notes from his school classmates.

"Thank you so much!" the mother said through tears, her daughter again translating. "It's a miracle that my son is alive."

"Oh, we rejoice with you!" the pastor replied. "God heard our cries for help that afternoon."

The group talked through the details of the accident: how Leonel had gone into the street chasing the family dog that had gotten loose, and how the impact of Leonel's head had left a major dent in the pickup's hood. Soon, however, the conversation turned to spiritual things. It happened to be mid-December, and so Pastor Eric said, "You know, this is the whole story of Christmas: God sent his Son to rescue us all from a terrible state. He came to conquer death, to give us life everlasting. We can have new hope because of what Jesus did for us."

Before the night was over, the entire family—including a grandfather who was present as well—prayed, inviting Christ into their hearts and lives.

A Public Celebration

Within two weeks, the boy was running around normally. Early in the new year, Pastor Eric invited them to share their story on a Sunday morning (at New Hope International Christian Church in Norwalk). Spread across the platform, the family smiled. "First of all, we want to say thank you to everyone who prayed," the mother began, with Brianda translating. "We are so thankful that our son survived."

The father added, "We know that our heavenly Father is true. We want to thank him. We met him at that moment."

Brianda then added, "Thanks to everybody who prayed for my brother, because the heavenly Father heard the prayers and is right here with us."

Pastor Eric extended the microphone toward Leonel. "Would you like to say anything?" he asked.

The boy simply said with a shy smile, "Thank you."

Contact with this family did not continue as long as everyone had hoped, due to the fact that soon after, their landlord decided to sell the property. The family was forced to move in with the wife's relatives some twenty miles away. Pastor Eric tried to connect with them but exchanges became sporadic, until finally, they opted to take more permanent shelter in a different state.

They still come back to LA occasionally for visits, and every time they stop to see the people who called on the name of Jesus for them that terrible Saturday. Leonel continues to grow tall and strong and has started to play soccer in his school—an ongoing testimony to the power of God's miraculous grace.

chapter 17

A CHURCH IN A BOXING RING?

If you go to church some Sunday morning at Grupo Unidad in downtown Tijuana, Mexico, you might not realize the building used to be a boxing ring. You'd be even more surprised to hear the backstory of how this congregation of nearly six thousand came to call this place home.

Four Catholic ladies back in the early 1980s, led by Maria Luisa Cuevas, began praying for a spiritual awakening in their city. They asked an evangelical pastor named Fermin Garcia Sr. (father of the current pastor) if he would be willing to stop by on Friday nights and teach them the Bible. Others wanted to hear as well, and the little group began to grow.

In time, the managing director of Unibanco, a major financial institution in Mexico, came along and offered to let them use an empty boxing arena on which his bank had foreclosed. Seating 3,500, it was far too big for their needs. But, if the fledgling church went in and at least did some cleanup, he would be pleased.

The little congregation, of no more than thirty people, took the banker up on his offer. With audacious faith, they began praying, "Lord, give us this place as our home." In fact, a prophecy in one meeting declared, "God has given you this place. From here, people will go out throughout the world to preach the gospel." Pastor Garcia and his flock kept meeting week after week, seeking to lead more people to Christ.

Two years passed. Then came the unwelcome news that a boxing promoter had succeeded in buying the arena from the bank, intending once again to hold fights there. He wanted the church out of his way.

Off to a rented downtown theater the group trekked. They wondered if the prophecy had been accurate. Had they perhaps misinterpreted it? They had no master plan; they could foresee no great future.

They were surprised, four years later, when the promoter got back in touch, asking for a meeting. "I need to sell this building, and I thought of you people," he began. "Would you be interested in coming back? I need $2 million for the property." (Business deals in the border city of Tijuana are usually quoted in American dollars rather than Mexican pesos, whose value tends to swing up and down more quickly.)

Mindful that his congregation numbered no more than four hundred worshipers at this point, Pastor Garcia replied honestly, "There's no way we could come up with that much money." The meeting ended fruitlessly.

A month later, the promoter called back. This time he was more forthright in admitting, "I've gotten into a financial bind with the Hacienda" (Mexico's tax authority), "and I really need to raise some cash. Can we talk again?" An appointment was set. The pastor and his son, plus another associate, would meet him outside the arena.

There in the sunshine, the man repeated his desire to sell.

The pastor replied, "Yes, I understand you've quoted a price of two million—but I don't have faith for that much."

"Well—what do you have faith for?" the man wanted to know.

Pastor Garcia answered very deliberately, "I will offer you $500,000—payable as $50,000 up front, then $200,000 when the sales contract is signed, $100,000 a year later, and $150,000 the final year. No interest! That is all we can do."

The man was quiet, staring at the pastor for a full minute. Would he wave them away? No one could tell what was going through his mind.

Finally, he spoke: "When can you give me the fifty?"

Pastor Garcia and the others let out the breaths they had been holding. "I can do it right now!" he answered. Within minutes he had called the church's treasurer to come meet them. She arrived with the checkbook and wrote out a $50,000 check on the spot.

The man took the check and then promptly handed over the keys. "It's yours," he announced.

Abundance from the Provider

From that moment forward, gifts to the church began to surge. Strangers would walk in off the street and push envelopes of money under the office threshold. The Garcias were amazed at how local funds came pouring in.

One older gentleman came calling without an appointment, asking to see the pastor. When told he was busy, the stranger said he would wait. Finally, a weary Pastor Garcia came out into the reception area. He expected to be asked for money, which happened often.

The man stood up. "Brother Garcia, I am excited to meet you," he began. "I am not from this church, but I heard that Christians were buying this building. And that excites me! So I came to give you a $5,000 offering."

As funds kept accumulating, it started to appear that the church would not need the full time to pay off the building. This goal could be achieved much sooner. A month into the process, $200,000 was available to sign the sales contract. Funds kept coming, raising hopes that the church might even be able to take advantage of a promised write-down of $50,000 for paying the full amount by year's end.

"The Lord spoke to my father during that season," the son remembers, "saying, 'Don't go to the Americans for money. I will be your Provider.' So often, Mexican pastors who want to expand their ministry appeal to their wealthier contacts up north. In this case, the Lord said not to do that."

Plans were developed for a grand opening celebration weekend. Feeling confident, Pastor Garcia invited many guest dignitaries, including two American pastor friends of his. He even volunteered to pay their airfares and hotel stays plus meals—an outlay that came to $3,000. The celebration was a great inspiration to all.

When all the offerings were counted and the sums totaled up, the entire building fund came to $197,000—nearly enough to pay the remaining balance all at once. Pastor Garcia could not help noticing, however, that the $3,000 shortfall was exactly what he had spent on entertaining the American guests. Apparently, the Lord's instruction to him should not have been ignored.

And the two American gifts were nowhere near what might have been expected. One pastor had written a check for $35, the other a check for $25. That was all—just $60.

And when deposited, both checks bounced!

"We still have those checks in our history vault," says Fermin Garcia Jr., chuckling. "They serve as a reminder not to stray from what the Lord says. When he says he will meet our needs in a certain way, he means it."

The following Wednesday, after the big weekend, the father was due to sign legal papers before a notary public (which in

Mexico functions as a full-fledged government attorney and recorder of transactions). On Tuesday, he closed himself off in prayer about the shortfall of $3,000. An hour later, the phone rang. A woman in Guadalajara, more than 2,200 kilometers southeast, said, "Brother Garcia, I heard you were buying that boxing arena, and I wanted to donate some money for it. I will wire it up to you."

Somewhat out of character, the pastor said hesitantly, "Could I ask you how much?"

"Yes—$5,000," she replied. This would cover the $3,000 that was lacking—plus the notary public's $2,000 fee. And as it turned out, the woman flew up to Tijuana that very night to give the money in person.

The church's growth and effectiveness since that time have continued to swell. Recently, the building was appraised at a value of $5.2 million. Several corporations have tried to buy it just to get the prime location, but the church presses on with its higher calling. Some forty daughter churches have been started in other parts of the city, in other Mexican cities such as Ensenada, and even across the border in San Diego, California, and Phoenix, Arizona.

"If we just have faith in a miracle-working God," says Fermin Garcia Jr. today, "he will build his church in his own way. We must learn to trust him far above the economic system. He will never fail."

chapter 18

MESSENGER AT THE REST STOP

Excitement was running high for grandmother-to-be Marcia Huff and her husband, Rick; just two more weeks, and the bundle of joy would be born. This would be their first grandchild, and they could hardly wait …

But then—the phone rang early one morning. "Mom, I haven't felt the baby move this morning!" their daughter Heather cried. "I didn't feel any movement last evening either, but I thought for sure I would today."

Marcia's medical training immediately kicked into gear. "Honey, that's not normal this late in the pregnancy. Get to your doctor right away."

"Well, I have an appointment tomorrow," Heather answered.

"No," Marcia said firmly. "Don't wait another minute. You must get checked out."

Within hours, another call conveyed the bad news: much of the amniotic fluid had leaked away, the baby had swallowed some of its meconium, and inducement would be started right away.

It took a day or two for Marcia and Rick to get free from their jobs so they could start driving the nearly one thousand miles from their southwest Missouri home toward Savannah, Georgia. The baby girl had been delivered by then and was not doing well. The grandparents intended to push straight across the country; they couldn't imagine stopping overnight somewhere. They needed to get to the East Coast as soon as possible.

"And wouldn't you know, we got into hard rain!" Marcia remembers. "It just wouldn't quit. In one place, the wind and rain were so strong a big tree had fallen right across the highway. We had to wait quite a while for that to be cleared. Then a little farther, there was a bad accident; traffic slowed to a crawl once again.

"I was so upset I said right out loud, 'God, you know what's going on here. You have control over the rain. Why don't you stop it?!'"

The long day eventually turned to night. Weariness sank in, but the couple pressed on. They simply had to get to their loved ones quickly.

Stranger in the Night

It was close to midnight when, somewhere in eastern Tennessee, Rick pulled off into a rest area. The place seemed quiet at this hour, except for one or two other cars. When Marcia entered the ladies' room, she saw an older African American woman standing at the mirror combing her beautiful silver-gray hair.

The two made eye contact in the mirror as Marcia reached out for the stall door handle. "But for some reason, I felt drawn to this woman," she remembers. "I turned to look at her again—and when I did, she motioned with her hand for me to come closer."

Marcia, in her distraught state, ended up falling into the older woman's arms. Soon the stranger began to pray aloud. Her volume kept rising as she besought God's help; eventually, she switched from English to an unknown tongue. The climax came when the woman ended her prayer and made a bold statement to Marcia:

"It's not going to look good at first. But it's going to be okay."

Marcia could only whimper, "My grandbaby, my grandbaby …"

"I understand," the stranger answered. "But it's going to be okay." And with that, she left the restroom.

An overwhelming peace settled upon Marcia in that moment. To this day, she doesn't remember whether she actually used the facilities or not. She only recalls exiting into the main area a few moments later—where her husband, who had been more or less standing guard for his wife outside the restroom door and listening to the rising volume, waited with a perplexed look on his face.

"What in the world was that all about?" he wanted to know. "I was just about to come in there!"

Marcia glanced around. "Did you see anyone come out just now?" she asked.

"Yes," he said. "There was this crazy woman! She had her hands in the air and she was talking to herself. She just took off; I don't know where she went."

Marcia stared at her husband. "Rick, she wasn't crazy," she said. "She was praying for us, and she told me something really great." Back on the road, Marcia proceeded to recite the whole exchange.

Was this a real human person sent to that rest area by the Lord? Or was she a heavenly being? To this day, Marcia honestly doesn't know. "Either way, the episode just increased our faith so much."

The Result

It was around six a.m. when the Huffs, still pushing through the rain, arrived at St. Joseph's/Candler Hospital in Savannah. They had to call their son-in-law's cell phone to help get past a security guard.

As the messenger had prophesied, new baby Shannon was

still in great peril. Doctors could not give much hope that she would survive. She had been rushed into the neonatal intensive-care unit (NICU) for more advanced care. The battle for her life raged on for several days.

"But, we held on in faith that God would keep his word," Marcia says. Finally, the medical prognosis began to improve. Some numbers were coming into range while others lagged. It took a while before Heather and her husband could take their daughter home.

Today, however, Shannon is a normal twelve-year-old living a healthy life. She and her parents have moved back to Missouri, where all three generations are active at Carthage Family Worship Center. "If I never see another miracle the rest of my life," says the grandmother, "I *know* I've seen at least one! She's my princess. And I'll tell her someday all about the lady God sent me in that restroom in the middle of the night, to build up my faith."

DIVINE ARREST

Certainly every urban church has to think about safety and security issues, both for its people and its property. Thieves, for example, would love to get their hands on a church's computers, microphones, video cameras—anything to sell on the street.

The 24,000-member West Angeles Church of God in Christ, which sits on Los Angeles' busy Crenshaw Boulevard just a few blocks south of the Santa Monica Freeway, prays about this constantly. It's a standing topic at the church's regular prayer meetings—which happen not just once a week but *three times daily*, at six a.m., twelve noon, and six p.m., seven days a week.

God's watchfulness showed itself, especially after the Sunday evening service on August 17, 2014, as worshipers were heading to their cars or waiting for LA Metro buses. Suddenly, gunfire erupted.

Head of security Officer Brandon Randall remembers his radio crackling to life a few seconds later. "Shots fired!" one of his guards yelled. "We've got a body down right at the front of the courtyard gate!" Randall immediately ran from the executive parking area, where he had been waiting for the church's well-known pastor, Bishop Charles E. Blake, to see what was happening at the main entrance to the cathedral.

There he found a young man face down, his feet still on the sidewalk while his upper body was sprawled inside the gate. His arms were spread out, and a handgun lay at his feet. Shattered glass littered the area; one of the church's front-facing windows had sustained a bullet hole.

"What happened?" Officer Randall wanted to know.

"He got shot!" a bystander said.

"No, he shot himself!" another person insisted.

"He just collapsed," a third person said. It was hard to know which story to believe.

The police soon arrived, followed by paramedics. Rolling the young man over, they found he was still breathing, though unresponsive. Quickly they cut open his shirt and other clothing, looking for bullet wounds. They found none.

Loading him onto a gurney, they raced away toward the nearest hospital with sirens blaring. The police, understandably, wanted to see the church's surveillance video. There, they identified this young man walking toward the entrance with a gun in his hand. As he tried to enter the church property, he suddenly dropped the firearm and fell to the ground. But, why?

It was the next day before Officer Randall and his staff got the rest of the story. As soon as the gurney had been wheeled into the ambulance and secured, the young man awakened. A more thorough examination by the hospital's ER doctor again found no bullet punctures. He appeared to be unharmed in any way. Nobody seemed to have a clue as to why his body had locked up on him.

They could only record the following on his medical chart: "An unexplained illness that caused a temporary comatose state."

Bishop Blake has a different explanation. "This was a miraculous fulfillment of Psalm 27:2–3 (NKJV)," he says.

When the wicked came against me
To eat up my flesh,
My enemies and foes,
They stumbled and fell.
Though an army may encamp against me,
My heart shall not fear;
Though war may rise against me,
In this I *will* be confident.

The pastor continues:

"Not only do I see a young man being arrested by God as a modern-day miracle, but I see a prophetic reminder of God's miraculous and glorious power. He has the ability to arrest us, to stop us in our tracks, and to cause us to fall prostrate in total surrender to his will.

"I am more than grateful to God for sparing the lives of the saints and those attending that church service. Whatever the Enemy meant for evil, God turned it around for the good!"

People—Christians and unbelievers alike—often wonder aloud why God doesn't reach down and stop bad happenings in our world.

Well … sometimes he does.[1]

chapter 20

'TWAS BLIND, BUT NOW ...

What do you do when you're a pediatric nurse, a busy single mom raising three adopted teenagers—and you start losing your eyesight?

That is the storm cloud that engulfed Elvira Higgins of Hollywood, Florida, in September 2004. A long-time diabetic, she had already lost partial vision in her right eye following an unsuccessful laser surgery. Now, all at once on one weekend, she lost 95 percent of the vision in her left eye, to the point that she couldn't even see her own fingernails. Obviously, she couldn't keep her job at Jackson Memorial Hospital, in nearby Miami. How would she provide for her kids—or even take care of herself?

Her only source of encouragement came from her spiritual family at Living Word Open Bible Church, where she was a choir member. "God's people prayed, and I believed he would carry me through somehow," she says, "even though Satan tried to make me doubt." She stayed faithful in attending services as often as she could get a ride. She also listened more often to Scripture recordings and Christian music at home.

Could laser surgery on her left eye possibly regain what had been lost? She opted to at least give it a try.

Associate Pastor Dyrie Francis remembers spotting Elvira one Sunday morning, sitting quietly on a bench outside the church. The woman's body language spoke clearly of dejection. "How are you today, sister?" the pastor said gently, sitting down beside her.

"Not so well," Elvira answered.

"What has happened? Tell me about it."

"Well ... I had another surgery on my 'good' eye this time," she began tearfully. "And it didn't work. The doctor says I'm legally blind now. There's no hope of ever seeing again.

"I'm trying to figure out all the things I'm going to have to change in this new way of living," she continued. "Getting around, shopping for the kids, making ends meet ... it's just overwhelming."

Pastor Francis hugged her close and said, "Oh, that is just so hard. I don't have answers for you—but I know we're going to pray and ask God to show up in this situation."

Time and again over the next six months, the church anointed her eyes with oil and prayed fervently for her healing. And not only on Sundays—this need was a standing request at the Tuesday morning prayer-and-fasting sessions. "Oh, God, we plead with you to help our dear sister!" they prayed. "She's in a terrible predicament."

As a step of faith, every day at home Elvira would open her Bible and try to read the page, only to lay it aside in frustration. How she wanted to review familiar verses such as Psalm 107:20— "He sent out his word and healed them; he rescued them from the grave"—or Isaiah 53:5—"But he was pierced for our transgressions, he was crushed for our iniquities; the punishment that brought us peace was on him, and by his wounds we are healed." But now she could only pray for her eyes while trying to remember the words.

The winter passed without any change. One Sunday morning in church, as Senior Pastor Karl Francis (Dyrie's husband) spoke,

Elvira turned her head in the direction of the voice, even though she couldn't see him. In that moment, a different voice arose in her head—the Holy Spirit asking, *So you have accepted your blindness?*

Elvira was startled. *No, Lord!* she silently replied. She wasn't sure what to expect next.

On the morning of Good Friday, March 25, 2005, she opened her Bible once again as usual. Staring at the page, she could suddenly read the words! Amazed and jubilant, she burst out in praise to God. She quickly called the church to cancel her ride to the Good Friday service later on. She spent the rest of the day rejoicing.

When Dyrie Francis met her in the sanctuary that evening, she was shocked. "Elvira—what happened?! How did you get here?"

"I drove myself! The Lord touched my eyes. I can see!" Dyrie was overcome with joy. The two women embraced and gave thanks to the God of all grace and blessing. That night, Pastor Karl invited Elvira to share her miracle of healing before a packed church. The congregation erupted in shouts of praise to God.

Elvira couldn't wait to make an appointment to see her doctor once again. The conversation in the examining room was priceless.

He: "There's no one with you today. How did you get here?"

She: "I drove myself!"

He: "No—that's impossible. You're blind!"

She: "Not anymore. Jesus made me see again!"

He: [Long pause … then finally] "This is amazing."

With his certification, plus a clearance from the employee health department, Elvira was welcomed back to her job. Before long, younger nurses were asking her to read the fine print on ampoules (sealed vials) of liquid medicine that they couldn't decipher.

Elvira Huggins is now in her late sixties and continues life with excellent vision. Not even glasses are needed. "Thank God for his unmerited love and plentiful grace and favor," she says. "He held on to me through trying times. He is still the Divine Healer."

chapter 21

THE MESSAGE GETS THROUGH

The apostle Paul clearly instructed the Corinthians that any display of public tongues in the church needed to be followed by an interpretation—otherwise, "how will anyone know what you are saying?"[1]

But, what if the hearers don't *need* an interpretation because they already understand the tongues?

That is what surprised a young pastor named E. C. McKinley one day around 1990, as he was just finishing a hospital call. He had gone to Kingsport, Tennessee's Holston Valley Medical Center to see one of his members from the small Church of God of Prophecy he served. On his way toward the exit, he noticed in the ICU waiting room, a cluster of agitated people all speaking Spanish—not a common sight in this Appalachian area. He could tell by the tears and hugs that something bad had happened.

Pastor McKinley didn't know any Spanish, so he waited on the edges until he heard a bit of English coming from one young woman. Approaching her, he gently asked, "What happened?"

"We were all in a group driving down from up north, and we

had this terrible accident!" she exclaimed. "My sister's in intensive care—we don't know if she's going to make it!"

"I'm so sorry," the pastor replied. "I'm a minister; is there anything I can do to help?"

"No, not really," she said. "The rest of the group is going to have to keep driving pretty soon, but my mother and I are going to stay here."

The pastor stepped away at that point to call his wife and ask for her assistance. After picking her up at home, they stopped at a store to buy some snacks and other things. The next day they returned to the hospital. Their gifts, along with the small amount of money he had in his wallet, were warmly appreciated.

"We wanted to help these dear folks in distress," he says, "but the language barrier with the mother was going to be hard to overcome."

By the third day, the gravely injured daughter remained in critical condition. When the pastor arrived in the ICU waiting area, he found the gray-haired mother sitting alone; thus, he would have no translator to help him. He tried to greet her with gestures. Through her continuing tears, she gave him a slight smile in return, apparently remembering the previous day's kindness of him and his wife.

"Let me pray for you," he said in English, folding his hands and bowing his head to pantomime his intent. "*Si*" ("Yes"), the woman replied.

Reaching out to take her hand, he began, "Lord, we come to you today in this hour of great need. You see the terrible thing that has happened to this dear woman's daughter. We need you to come and be the Great Physician here in this hospital. In your love and grace, reach down and touch her in the ICU. Come, Lord Jesus, and show your mighty power in this situation." By now, the woman was sobbing almost inconsolably.

After a few minutes, Pastor McKinley switched over to speaking in tongues. After all, the woman couldn't understand his English anyway, so what did it matter? The longer this went on, the more boldly the woman began to call out, *"Si! Si! Si!"* The pastor continued for some time in a language of the Spirit.

When he finished, she reached out to embrace him, still weeping. Just then, he turned around to see that the bilingual daughter had returned to the waiting room and had been listening.

"I thought you couldn't speak Spanish!" she said.

The pastor was shocked. "I—I don't," he answered.

"Yes, you do!"

"No, really—I don't," he protested.

"You just told my mother that Christ died for her sins. You said she only needed to receive him as her Lord, and she would be saved. And so, that's how my mother was praying just now!"

Like on the original day of Pentecost, the gospel had been conveyed in a tongue the hearer could readily understand, even if the speaker could not. As a result, a distressed soul had been brought into the family of God.

That very afternoon, the daughter in ICU woke up from her coma. By the next day, she was moved to a regular hospital room. Not long after, when Pastor McKinley came again to visit, he found she had been discharged. The threesome had quickly resumed their travel southward, making further contact unfeasible.

"But I've never forgotten the powerful surprise of that day in the waiting room," he says. "Nothing about it was preplanned on my part. God the Holy Spirit just moved in to meet a particular need. He knew what he wanted to accomplish, and he used the instrument of tongues to reach his goal."

chapter 22

WHEELCHAIR NO MORE

Young Jeff Moore used to play on a wheelchair basketball team. He doesn't anymore. So what happened?

Tim Stafford, senior writer for *Christianity Today*, tells the story at the opening of his insightful 2012 book entitled *Miracles: A Journalist Looks at Modern-Day Experiences of God's Power*.

Jeff Moore was a high school student in my church, a dark-haired, good-looking teenager, with paper-white skin and a slight build. He was well liked, polite, quiet but friendly. He never drew attention to himself or his problem.

Jeff had lost the use of his feet—they hurt so much that they would no longer carry his weight. He came to church in a wheelchair.

I didn't know Jeff or his family then, but I often saw them at morning worship. I attend a Presbyterian church with about six hundred members. It is a warm, Bible-believing, multi-generational church that is a little traditional but tries to be flexible. We sing hymns with an organ, but we also try to bridge the gap between generations by using contemporary songs with a band. Jeff's mother, Sheri, was one of a handful of worship leaders very visibly singing in the choir at the front of the church.

Jeff was visible because he was the only young person in a wheelchair. Every week his father wheeled him into church. It could not have been easy to come to church that way, and their faces showed the strain, I thought. Yet Jeff was always present with his parents and his two younger brothers.

It made me sad to see this healthy young man so crippled. It brought mystification, too. I had never heard of a young person whose feet hurt so much he couldn't walk. Why couldn't doctors figure it out? Somebody told me his case baffled them.

Then one Sunday morning, our pastor announced that Jeff's mother had something to share. Sheri stepped out of the choir and quietly said that Jeff had been healed. He had gone to a service at a church in another city, several hours away, and after healing prayer, he stepped out of his wheelchair. His pain was completely gone. He could walk. He could run. God had healed him, his mother said.

I heard several spontaneous expressions of praise—two or three exclamations of "Praise the Lord!" Later in the service, our pastor prayed and thanked God for what he had done for Jeff. But truthfully, the response was restrained. No whooping. No delirious thanks. And not a lot of buzz afterward. Maybe—and here I might be projecting my own feelings—there was some uncertainty as to how we should react.

I heard that Jeff's family was disappointed by the response. They had been bubbling over with joy, but they weren't met with the same emotions.

Why the restraint? I'm guessing at what others felt, because there wasn't any public discussion. I know what I felt, and I suspect it was typical.

I was very glad at Jeff's news, but I was hesitant to put too much weight on it. I didn't know what had caused Jeff's problem, but it seemed possible it was psychosomatic. The mind is a very tricky thing. What if we whooped it up over a miracle and then discovered that the problem came back days or weeks later? That wouldn't put God in a very good light. It wouldn't build anybody's faith.

I also worried about Jeff being disappointed. Sometimes people want so much for God to heal them that they convince themselves he has done so. But the problem doesn't really disappear. It comes back, and eventually the hurting person has to face reality—no miracle. Then he or she is left wondering why God put them through such high hopes and disappointment. …

As it turned out, those fears were misplaced in Jeff's case. Months later he was bouncing around like any other young man, utterly pain-free. He really was healed.

What does that say about those of us who hesitated? Was it a judgment on our lack of faith?

I wasn't very happy when I heard the reaction from the pastor at the church where Jeff was healed. He told his congregation about Jeff's healing with great jubilation—as he should have. Then he added, with equal jubilation, "A Presbyterian church in the Bay Area had its faith rocked!" and his congregation roared.

The implication seemed to be that stodgy Presbyterians had a few lessons to learn, as though miracles were a contest, with winning churches and losing churches.

That stuck in my craw a bit. But I had to admit I was envious of the pastor's self-assurance. …

I long to see God's life in the world. I want to know where he's at work. I want to cooperate with him in the way he chooses to operate. I want to walk by his side, working with him. But I want it to be real—not hyped-up fantasy faith.

Nearly three years after Jeff's healing, I decided to talk to him. Jeff's story had stayed in my mind. Why couldn't a Christian congregation—*my* congregation—celebrate such a wonderful healing with heart and soul? Why had Jeff received such a muted and mixed response?

Also, I wanted to know exactly what had happened to Jeff and his family. Had the healing been complete? In the years since, had pain returned?

I found Jeff's number in the church directory, called him up, and explained that I would like to hear his story. Jeff's voice over the phone was hesitant. He said he wasn't sure. I didn't press him, I just emphasized how much I would like to hear what had happened to him and asked him to think it over.

After that, I hung up. Was there something embarrassing that he didn't want to share? Had pain come back to his feet? I hadn't seen him at church lately; it could be because we attended different services, but it could be something more troubling.

I had to leave several messages before I reached him again, and this made me wonder even more. But when I finally got through, Jeff agreed to talk.

I met him at a local coffee shop and almost didn't recognize him. I remembered him as slight and pale, but he had become tanned and strong.

His manner struck me even more. Jeff isn't a talker. He didn't volunteer details about his healing. Truthfully, he wasn't eager to talk about anything that far in the past. He had moved on, and that actually made his story more believable. Jeff was not selling anything. There wasn't a trace of hype in his manner. He was a just-the-facts guy.

Apparently he had been that way even when he was disabled. From what he said, he hadn't worked himself into a fever, praying for healing for his damaged feet. On the contrary, after five years of constant medical interventions—five separate surgeries, countless doctors' appointments, acupuncture, physical therapy, orthotics—he had just wanted to be left alone.

The problem with his feet had snuck up on him gradually. The Moores were an active, adventurous family. They back-packed, they hiked, they took up some kind of outdoor activity virtually every weekend. When Jeff was nine or ten, he began to complain about his feet when the family went hiking. His parents thought it was his boots.

After a family trip to the county fair, Jeff complained that his feet were killing him. His parents thought nothing of it. Who doesn't have hurting feet after walking around the fair all day?

When he was thirteen, Jeff had an accident on his skateboard, but instead of healing, his foot stayed swollen. Eventually he went to the doctor, who told him he had broken something called a tarsal coalition. Jeff had flat feet, and to make up for the lack of flexibility in his feet, his body had fused together some of the bones. When Jeff fell off his skateboard, the "fusion" had broken, so the doctors put Jeff in a cast to allow the break to heal.

But the bones didn't heal, and the pain continued.

The surgeons cut open his foot and put in a titanium peg. The surgery worked as intended—his foot developed an arch—but after a long recuperation, Jeff still felt severe pain. Six months later they operated on the other foot, with the same result. Jeff described his story to me.

> I have a jar at home filled with all the screws they put in and later took out. In the last operation they cut open my calf and lengthened the muscle, slit my heel, slid it over, and tried to remake my foot. [This elaborate surgery required Jeff to spend six months in a cast, and relearn how to walk with his altered foot.] They succeeded, in a way. They really did form perfect arches. I no longer had flat feet. But the pain was still there.
>
> I could walk a little, but the more walking I did the more it hurt, until it was unbearable.

By the time I was seventeen I was done with it. They wanted to do another surgery, something drastic that would fuse my bones together. But after five surgeries and nothing different, I just gave up on it. I went for acupuncture and electrical stimulation, but they didn't help, either.

I was trying to accept that I was always going to be in a wheelchair. My parents were broken up by it, I think. They never really gave up hoping that I could walk again. I have an aunt whom I've never met, who gave money to a church that prayed for me every week. They sent me a card telling me that they had prayed for me. I thought it was kind of odd, to tell you the truth. Nobody else prayed for me, that I knew of, and I'm not sure how I would have felt about it if they had offered. I definitely did not believe that healing could happen.

I wasn't really mad about it. Some days I was fine, some days I was just irritable. I wanted to forget about change and deal with what was going to be my life.

By that time, Jeff was attending the local junior college, pulling his wheelchair out of the back of his classic Mustang and rolling himself in and out of classes. At an adaptive PE class, he struck up a friendship with another student named Leland, who was also in a wheelchair. Leland was older than Jeff and covered in tattoos. He had lost the use of his legs years before. A very friendly guy, Leland invited Jeff to join a wheelchair basketball team.

The first time Jeff attended a practice, he came home elated in a way he had not been for years. He loved the all-out way they played, smashing into each other, even knocking each other out of their wheelchairs. Practice soon became his favorite day of the week. It was great to get physical.

When the team entered a tournament in Redding, a four-hour

drive away, Jeff's parents were concerned. Leland had offered to drive, but they didn't know him, and the trip would necessitate staying overnight in a motel.

"Right," Jeff said to their worries. "How many mass murderers do you know who are confined to a wheelchair?"

Seeing how much it meant to Jeff, they let him go.

Jeff found the tournament enjoyable, even though one of his teammates had a terrible seizure and had to be taken away by ambulance. The games wrapped up on Saturday night. On Sunday morning, Leland suggested to Jeff that they go to a church he knew. Jeff had no objection, so they wheeled their chairs into a sprawling structure known as Bethel Church. Jeff sat through the service and wasn't particularly struck by it.

After the service they invited people who wanted prayer to come forward. Leland wanted us both to go. I wouldn't have done it without his urging. I was not really hoping for anything, but I wheeled down to the front because Leland urged me. Two young people came up and prayed for us, laying hands on us. We weren't the center of attention. Other people were praying nearby.

I didn't feel anything while they prayed, and I really didn't think anything had happened. Then one of them said, "Jeff, stand up."

I did stand up. That was nothing special. I could always stand. I waited for the pain to start, as it always did. But this time it didn't. I took a few steps. No pain. Somebody suggested I should do something that would really hurt. I walked up on the stage, four feet high, and jumped to the ground. That should have been excruciating, but there was no pain. None. From that moment, I've never had another ounce of pain in my feet.

I was in shock. Most people had already left the church, but we hung around awhile, talking to people.

Jeff had spoken to me in a very matter-of-fact voice, but at this moment his eyes went into space. His words came out quietly, dreamily. "I'll always remember pushing my wheelchair down the aisle and out of that church."

Jeff didn't call his parents. They had no idea what had happened when he reached home that afternoon. "Mom, Dad, guess what," he said, getting out of the car. "My feet aren't hurting." As she absorbed the news, his mom began to cry. Typical of Jeff, he didn't want to talk about it. He grabbed his skateboard. He hadn't used it in years, but he still remembered how.

Jeff's feet were like new, but his legs were the same old legs. He hadn't used them for years, and the muscles had atrophied. Skateboarding soon wore him out; walking was hard. His legs were so sore he had to use crutches for several days.

When he went to class on Monday, everybody wanted to know what had happened to him. All the years he had been in a wheelchair, nobody ever asked questions. Now he told the story over and over again. "The reactions were mixed. I could tell that some people just didn't believe me. Others were amazed. At church, reactions were also mixed. Many people were overjoyed. All my friends thought it was just awesome. But I could tell a lot of people didn't know what to think."

Jeff didn't begrudge anybody their doubts. "If it had been reversed, I would have been the same way."

It is curious to note that Jeff's friend Leland, who had brought him to the church and received the same prayer ministry, was not healed as a result. In a later chapter, Tim Stafford reflects:

I'm convinced that, for Jeff Moore, a miracle took place at Bethel Church. I'm convinced partly because of the kind of person he is—no hype, no guile—but I'm also convinced by the astonishing turnaround. To go from crippling pain to no pain at all in the instant that praying hands were laid on him seems unexplainable in medical terms. (His surgeon takes the same view. When asked how he explains Jeff's condition, he simply says, "A miracle.")

This is a "sign and wonder," to use biblical terminology. But the sign doesn't seem to communicate the same thing to everybody. If you think miracles prove God, you can't help but notice that not everybody responds to the proof. Jeff told anybody who was interested what had happened to him, but some didn't believe him. Even people at his own church had their doubts. …

From Jeff's experience, I learned that such things happen. They really do. They don't happen very often—if they did, we wouldn't call them miracles. But they do happen, and that gives me great encouragement.

Stafford concludes his book with these three paragraphs:

Miracles are wonderful gifts from God, but they also bring temptations. Satan knew that when he tempted Jesus, offering him the chance to do miracles. Jesus passed the test by *not* doing miracles, because that was not what God had called him to do at that moment.

We are tempted to seek kingdom, power, and glory for ourselves. But not even Jesus would take them for himself. To God only belong the kingdom and the power and the glory. He is the miracle worker.

It is in God's very nature to astonish us by his goodness. He does wonders as he wishes, in complete freedom. And we—we ask. We watch. We witness and express our grateful thanks.[1]

chapter 23

DOUBLE TROUBLE, DOUBLE PORTION

Jeff Farmer stepped off a regional jet at Mahlon Sweet Airport on the outskirts of Eugene, Oregon, in March 1988. The pungent odor from sawmill smokestacks was a vivid reminder of the Northwest and his college years in this place. Two decades had now passed. Once he was a student here; today he would be welcomed as the seventh president of his alma mater, a sixty-three-year-old Bible college.

No longer a single, two-story cement block building heated by sawdust, the picturesque twenty-acre campus of Eugene Bible College (EBC) now welcomed students and visitors along a winding road lined with stately pines. Nestled quietly in the southwest hills of the city, EBC overlooked the southern tip of the Willamette Valley, not far from the Oregon Trail terminus. The verdant green was a harbinger of spring in the Emerald Empire.

But the wonder was short-lived. Within hours, the board chairman was saying, "Jeff, there's good news: we recently retired the mortgage on the property and buildings. But enrollment is down, the budget is $50K in the red, and major repairs, maintenance, and capital expansion are desperately needed."

An inner voice roared, *Jeff, what have you gotten yourself into? You sensed the call of God to EBC—but did that rule out the wisdom of asking a few simple questions first?*

Reality intruded as Jeff began to reason: *Fundraising will be tough. Most graduates are in ministry, so the alumni association will not have an abundance of wealthy donors. Plus, I have no business contacts in this area. I haven't been here for twenty years. My friends have moved. What have I done?*

A Word in Season

Jeff faced these challenges alone for the moment, as his wife and children were still 1,800 miles away in Wichita, Kansas, finishing the school year and selling their house. His anxiety yielded to prayer, however, knowing that problems are raw materials in the hands of God for a miracle. And that is what the college surely needed—not one but several.

The spring quarter launched with 118 students. President Farmer preached the opening chapel service. The rest of the spring chapel schedule was already filled, including something called "Spiritual Growth Conference." It was to be a time when classes were dismissed to allow the entire college community to seek the Lord for a visitation of his refreshing presence and power.

A seasoned and highly recognized prophet named Dick Mills had been scheduled nearly two years in advance to headline the conference. Faculty and staff spoke highly of his prophetic insight and gifting. From hundreds of scriptural promises he had memorized, the Holy Spirit would quicken two or three for an in-the-moment "word of knowledge," which he would then impart to individuals he pointed out in the congregation.

The week began strongly with worship, prayer, and fasting. Dick Mills was well received. On the final day of the conference, he singled out Jeff and asked him to come to the platform. No one knew what would happen next.

"God has given me a word for you as the new president," the guest began. Soon he homed in on an obscure Scripture—the first half, and only the first half, of Job 11:6. "God," he said, "is about to show you 'the secrets of wisdom, that they are double to that which is'" (KJV). The sense of divine anointing was weighty in the chapel. Jeff took this public declaration to mean God would give divine wisdom to direct the college. He left that day encouraged in the Lord, confident he was in the center of God's will.

Thereafter, God's surprises began to fall like dominoes. And they did not stop for seven years.

A Bad Idea?

In an administrative meeting, Jeff proposed an initiative he felt certain the Lord had given him—to launch a $50,000 scholarship fund for women in ministry. It would be named for Senethea Meyer, EBC's first graduate in 1926. Now seventy-four years young, Senethea had poured half a century into the college as a teacher, registrar, bursar, bookstore manager, fundraiser, alumni association director, and always a vigilant prayer warrior. Short and slender, she was arguably the most animated member of the college staff. She said she didn't need anything personally, since the only two loves of her life were "Jesus and Eugene Bible College."

"When I proposed the Senethea Meyer Golden Scholarship Fund," Jeff recalls, "I thought my team would enthusiastically cheer. They all loved and respected Senethea, recognizing the value she had added to the institution."

The idea, however, fell to the floor with a thud. "The timing is all wrong," people argued. "We could never pull that off."

"Even if you could raise the money," the academic dean insisted, "it should go elsewhere where the needs are more desperate."

This was Jeff's first test as president. His calling, credibility, faith, and wisdom were all on the line. Should he back down in light of the counsel of valued team members? Was this a test of his obedience to the Lord?

In the days following, the Holy Spirit quickened to his mind Peter's response to the chief priest: "We must obey God rather than men."[1] So, he pressed forward. To the amazement of many, the $50,000 was raised quickly and presented as an endowed scholarship fund to an overwhelmed Miss Meyer.

"Each year until your promotion to heaven," Jeff explained that day, "you will assist the financial aid department in selecting a qualified female student for the scholarship." Nothing could have made her more grateful, nor crowned her life and ministry with grander celebration. Senethea's golden anniversary at the college was a memorable jubilee.

Just days later, a phone call came from missionary alumnus Gerine Snyder.

"President Farmer, I have been named the executor of the Warren Moore estate. He and his wife were EBC graduates and missionaries to Cuba. They have left $50,000 for the college to endow a scholarship fund for students majoring in missions."

Two sets of $50,000 may not sound like large sums to a well-endowed university, but to a small Bible college struggling to survive, it was an enormous amount of money. Who would have predicted that the word of knowledge about "secrets of wisdom … they are double to that which is" would take such literal shape?

And God's grace and provision were not finished yet.

Kitchen Craziness

Still basking in the glow of these twin miracles, Jeff's wife, Ramona, was making a cake for her dessert-loving husband one afternoon. Suddenly, he heard a shout from the kitchen.

He dashed to see what was wrong. "My cake might be ruined!" his wife cried as she wiped her flour-covered hands on her apron. "This is impossible!"

"What's wrong, honey?"

"It's the eggs," she replied. "I can't believe it! This whole carton is a mess. Every single egg I've cracked open so far has a double yolk, and my recipe doesn't call for two yolks. I keep thinking the next egg will be normal, so I keep trying … and here they are again—two instead of one!"

It was a "God" moment. And before the day was over, the Holy Spirit had caused Ramona to see the significance of the doubling miracle. She explained it to Jeff, and the light bulb in his head finally came on—*the eggs were a parable of divine wisdom, demonstrating God's intervention to launch a second $50,000 gift, to follow on the heels of the first one.*

Does God have such a sense of humor that he uses eggs? Chickens lay double-yolk eggs about once in a thousand times, the poultry experts say. Now, consider the odds of *twelve* such eggs ending up in the same carton. Then, consider the odds of that specific carton ending up in Eugene, Oregon … and the odds of it being placed for sale in a Fred Meyer grocery store, instead of in the Safeway or Albertson's down the road. Finally, multiply that by the odds of Ramona selecting that specific carton among the many others in the cooler, not to mention dozens of other shoppers who could have chosen it first.

God was making a statement. He was confirming his word.

But Wait! There's More . . .

This was not the end of the story. Jeff and his wife had no way of knowing God was launching seven years of divine initiatives clothed in miraculous double increases. While all of the increases were amazing blessings, we'll look at two of them more closely.

In 1990, EBC launched a campaign to build a new library-office-classroom building. The target for funding was $640,000, not including volunteer labor and support. The building was erected and dedicated debt-free.

Elated but exhausted, Jeff had no interest in considering another capital expansion project anytime soon. His professional judgment warned against it, if for no other reasons than personal burnout and donor fatigue.

However, God had other plans. The following year, a beautiful apartment complex for married students was built. The financing for the building was provided by a wealthy businessman in the community, who used a portion of his retirement funds for the project. And, after the architect and general contractor were paid, the final price was virtually identical to the cost of the last building constructed—$640,000. Further, once the complex was completed, all of the apartments were rented immediately, and the income they produced provided a generous positive cash flow for the college—another double by divine initiative.

Prayer Prevails

Then, in 1992, the college's neighbor, a medical doctor and his wife, were asking themselves what to do with their more than twenty-three acres of pristine, forested hillside property. They were weary of paying the property taxes and felt it might be time to scale back.

Any developer would drool to acquire the land. If subdivided into home sites, it would produce millions. But Dr. Greer was a Lutheran believer and a good neighbor of the college; so, he called President Farmer with a proposal.

"I have land adjacent to your campus," he said. "I would like to sell twenty acres to EBC for $10,000 per acre. I will carry the mortgage if you will give me 10 percent down—in other words, $20,000."

Shocked, Jeff whispered a prayer, then, answered transparently. "Dr. Greer, thank you for your consideration. You are catching me by surprise. Would you be willing to give me a week to pray about this and get back to you?"

"That would be fine, Jeff." And the call ended. Jeff hung up the phone knowing full well EBC did not have an extra $20,000 for a down payment. But he also knew if the college did not buy the property, a developer would swallow it up, and the school would be surrounded by traffic and houses instead of forest and nature—not a day went by without deer grazing on the campus slopes.

Jeff asked two people to pray with him: his wife and a mentor, Rev. R. J. "Bob" Haynes. Meanwhile, he attempted no fundraising. The trio simply prayed.

Four years had passed since the first "egg miracle." Now, however impossible it may sound, Ramona discovered another carton of eggs in her refrigerator with not one, not two, not three, but all twelve eggs with double yolks. Every single egg … again!

What could this signify? Was God at work to double the current campus from twenty acres to forty? The answer came, just before the seven-day time frame expired, when Bob Haynes called. "Jeff, I have a friend in California who would like to donate the down payment." Within months, the campus was twice as large as it had been.

While these three double miracles were the most significant to the college, EBC experienced other double increases during the seven years that further blessed and confirmed God's promise—the doubling of student enrollment, the doubling of professors with doctoral degrees, the doubling of smaller capital expansion projects, and the doubling of vehicle acquisitions.

The God who gave Job "twice as much as he had before"[2] and gave Elisha a double portion of his mentor's spirit[3] is the same God we serve today. His heart to bless us and enlarge our capacity is a recurring theme throughout the centuries.

chapter 24

A PROMISE KEPT

Susan Lowry, age twenty-three, had been married only a year when her body mysteriously went into revolt. All energy seemed to drain out of her while waves of nausea swept in on a daily basis. She began losing weight at an alarming rate. Her pulse, on the other hand, skyrocketed. She thought, *What in the world is going on?*

In June 1981, she managed to summon enough strength to attend a women's retreat in the Ozark Mountains, which her mother was directing. Everyone could tell something was seriously wrong with Susan. During a morning session in the chapel, the leader asked her to come to the platform for prayer. A group gathered around her and began to intercede as she held onto the pulpit to keep from collapsing.

A strong sense of God's presence seemed to sweep the room. One woman in a row near the front gave out a message in tongues. The chapel was quiet then, awaiting the interpretation in English. The same lady then followed with these words: "I am the Lord your God. I have heard your prayers. I am with you. Satan has buffeted you, but if you will only believe, you will be healed. I will make you completely whole … ." There were a few more sentences, but the entire interpretation lasted no more than one minute. The assembly then gave thanks for this direct word from the Spirit.

For the next week, Susan's health rebounded dramatically. "I was my old self!" she recalls. "I even went on a bus trip with my husband, Larry, and a group all the way to North Carolina. We spent some days at a mountain retreat, went hiking in the great outdoors, and also stopped in Cleveland, Tennessee, to tour our Church of God of Prophecy headquarters. I felt great!"

Once back home in Arkansas, however, her energy plunged again. All the old symptoms returned with a vengeance. Larry—a busy state youth director—would sometimes have to stay home and carry her from place to place. She even needed his help to get dressed and comb her hair. The young couple had no medical diagnosis at this point but pled with God to bring back the healing.

"I felt in my heart that maybe God had given me that one week of strength to show me that I *was* going to recover. But apparently, he was going to put me through a longer process first. We kept holding on to the promise from the women's retreat."

Hard Facts

Not long afterward, her physical condition weakened to the point that she entered North Little Rock Memorial Hospital. There, the physicians declared specific names for what was tormenting her—a toxic combination of a form of leukemia; sarcoidosis, which is an incurable inflammation of the lungs; and an extremely hyperactive thyroid that was producing four times the normal output. No wonder her weight was now down to eighty-five pounds while her heart was pounding away at more than two hundred beats per minute.

"I really don't know what's keeping you from congestive heart failure," one doctor admitted. "You're burning more calories lying in bed than a healthy person running a marathon."

While the medical experts struggled to find effective treatments, Susan and Larry concentrated on what God had said, both in the Bible and at the retreat through the gift of interpretation. Larry would read the Word to his wife, especially Psalm 27 ("Hear my voice when I call, LORD; be merciful to me and answer me. … Your face, LORD, I will seek. … I remain confident of this; I will see the goodness of the LORD in the land of the living. … Wait for the LORD."[1]).

Susan would personalize specific promises of God—for example, Psalm 107:20 MEV, which she recited as, "He sent out his word and healed [me], and delivered [me] from [my] destruction." Another anchor point became Mark 11:23–24, which are Jesus' words about believers being empowered to cast great mountains (of sickness!) in the sea.

That year, her twenty-fourth birthday landed on Father's Day. Her dad, Eddie Mounce (the denomination's state overseer), stopped by early that morning. Finding his daughter asleep, he chose not to awaken her but sat quietly for some minutes. Finally, she woke up. He kissed her and wished her, "Happy Birthday," to which she replied, "Happy Father's Day."

After he had left for church, Susan remarked to the patient in the other bed, "That was really sweet of my dad just to sit here quietly beside me, not even waking me up."

"Well," said the roommate, "he wasn't just sitting there. He was praying for you the entire time."

Still, her physical condition kept deteriorating, to the point that she could not even get out of the hospital bed without assistance. It was about this time that an unusual visitor came into her hospital room, she says: the Angel of the Lord. "He was very tall, with broad shoulders. He stood at the foot of my bed, never speaking. I could see just enough of his outline to know who he was. It reminded me of a Scripture I had memorized as a young girl: 'The angel of the LORD encampeth round about them that fear him, and delivereth them.' "[2]

When later that day she told her mother, Genelle, what had occurred, she quickly identified this as the Angel of the Lord, based on her own experience of seeing the same person, early one morning on her back porch, while praying for her daughter. She had feared this might be what is sometimes called "the death angel."[3] But the Lord assured her that Susan was heading not toward death but toward future ministry for his own purposes and glory. Once again, the interpretation of tongues was supported.

Wait, Wait

The doctors, however, were not nearly so optimistic. At the end of two weeks, they discharged Susan, telling Larry and the rest of the family simply to "make her comfortable" because there was nothing else they could do for her. Back at home, declarations of trust in an almighty God continued regardless. Relatives came from out of state to lend their prayer support.

Still, there was no positive news. During a church conference in July, Susan was able to attend but lay in a lawn chair the entire time, not even able to sit up and greet her friends. By August, she and Larry were praying, "Lord, could we have just one sign of improvement? It's getting to be a long time since the promise at the women's retreat. We need a glimmer of hope, please."

The next blood test at the hospital lab showed numbers moving in a better direction! Subsequent analyses and tests were taken. Every day seemed to bring a higher energy level. Once the healing began to evidence itself, Susan rapidly improved, to the point that she was back to full health by September—with no additional medical interventions or treatment.

Months later, when she went for a chest X-ray, there was no

sign of scarring on her lungs. Normally, sarcoidosis leaves scars even if somehow arrested from taking the person's life.

Today, more than three decades later, she is an active and healthy pastor's wife in Douglasville, Georgia, just west of Atlanta. She has told her healing story again and again in churches and women's gatherings. "I held onto the Holy Spirit's promise through that message," she always says. "I refused to doubt God's word given to me, personally. This supernatural gift of the Spirit sustained me and built faith inside me to wait upon the Lord until the healing became visible. To God be the glory!"

chapter 25

WHEN "NO" BECAME "YES"

Pastor John Penton and his wife, Linda, were in a deep financial hole and not sure how they would ever get out of it. They had poured nearly every cent they had into a start-up effort called Outreach Church of God in Christ in Bremerton, Washington—a navy town, of some forty thousand, across Puget Sound from Seattle.

"We really believed God wanted us to reach people for Christ—navy guys working at the big shipyard and longtime residents as well," he says. "We met for a while in a rented dance hall, which meant cleaning up the place every Sunday morning after all the carousing from the night before. But it was worth the effort."

Enough people were coming and the offerings seemed strong enough that John stepped out in faith and quit his job at the Tacoma Police Department (thirty miles south) to go full-time into the ministry. But as the months went on, the ends didn't meet. Several solid givers in the congregation got transferred by the navy and attendance slumped. The Pentons wound up using all their savings.

"We didn't want to give up," John says. "So—wisely or unwisely—we borrowed money against our house equity. But, it was an adjustable-rate loan, and the rates kept rising that year, to the point that we couldn't keep up. The bank foreclosed on us, forcing us and our three teenage kids out into a rental."

As if the church burden wasn't enough, John and Linda faced

the additional prospect of college bills just ahead. At least their two daughters and one son were high academic achievers and strong athletes; so, they hoped they could get scholarships.

That summer, the family borrowed an RV from a friend and decided to go looking at possible schools. Face-to-face contacts with the admissions departments might help the kids get a foot in the door better than just mailing in applications. They traveled from campus to campus, all the way to the East Coast.

While checking out Hampton University in Virginia, they went on Sunday to visit St. John's Church of God in Christ, in Newport News. The service was encouraging. But what really surprised them was what happened afterward as the family was getting back into the RV.

"A lady came walking over to say something to us there in the parking lot," John Penton remembers. "We were total strangers to her, of course. But she was on a mission as she said these words: 'God wanted me to tell you folks something. You are going to come into some money—so don't be afraid!'

"My wife and I were amazed, to say the least. We thanked her for this word of prophecy and then went on our way. Of course we had no idea how this might possibly come true."

A Name from the Past

Back home in the Northwest, John felt he had no choice but to go back into police work. Discouraged, he turned the Bremerton church over to another pastor and settled into the photo-and-fingerprinting tasks he had done before.

One day at work, the phone rang. An attorney up in Bremerton introduced himself and said, "I have an elderly client who wants to talk to you. His name is Bill Larsen. He says he trusts you and wants you to have power of attorney over his estate. When can you come up to my office and meet with the two of us?"

John Penton recognized the name instantly. This was a rather unusual man who years before had refused to sell him a piece of land for the church. John remembered eyeing this ten-acre plot, finding out that the owner lived alone on the property, and going out to approach him. "The house was unkempt and from the outside looked vacant," he says. "I went up to the front door and knocked. There was no reply. I failed to notice a rough sign that read I WILL SHOOT ANY RAT THAT STEPS ONTO MY PROPERTY!!!

"When I reached out to see if the doorknob would turn, I got an electric shock! He had apparently rigged up some kind of wiring to let people know he meant business."

The man inside did, however, come peeping through the curtain to see who was there.

"Hello!" John called out. "I'm a pastor from down the road, and we're looking to buy some property. I was wondering if I could talk to you about—"

"No!" the man thundered back. "I'm not selling!"

In the days and weeks following, however, the pastor kept trying to at least get to know this eccentric man, who was then somewhere in his seventies. "After one of our church dinners, we took him some of the leftover food," he says. "I kept inviting him to church. Sooner or later, he began showing up on Sunday.

"We actually got to be friends. I found out he had been a bluegrass musician, playing banjo and violin. So I took him to a few bluegrass concerts. That was a new experience for me; I learned a lot!

"I would drive him to his doctor appointments. At tax time each spring, I took him to see the tax preparation people.

"And best of all, he got to the point of giving his heart to the Lord. His gruff demeanor softened; we saw him smile more.

"But, he still wouldn't sell us his property!"

Together Again

Now the two men met again in the attorney's office. They greeted each other warmly. The attorney began talking through the legal details of making John Penton the financial manager of Bill's assets and executor of his estate. (On the side, the attorney confessed to John, "I wouldn't normally being doing this, but you held prayer meetings in my mother's home years ago. So I guess you're 'one of the good guys.' ")

The upshot of this arrangement was that Bill's finances became an open book to John. There he learned that Bill *had* sold the ten acres to a senior-living company after all, with the provision that Bill could stay in his place as long as he wished. The sizable proceeds of the sale had been deposited in a bank (the same bank that had foreclosed on the Pentons' house!).

Bill's investment advisers suggested to John that the man's money could do better if put into real estate, rather than just sitting in a savings account. When John discussed the option with Bill, he was open to the idea. The result was the purchase of a residence in Tacoma, titled in Bill's name, into which the Pentons would move and pay rent back to the estate.

"I really questioned the attorney," says John, "about whether this was entirely proper. I didn't want people in town gossiping that this black preacher was taking advantage of this old white guy. But the attorney said, 'No, don't worry about that at all. He tells everybody he meets, "I have full confidence in John. He's my friend." ' "

Subsequently, the Pentons offered to buy the house. When they all met once again with the attorney, John said, "Bill, you don't want to do that, do you? I thought you told me you wanted to *give* the house to these people once you're gone, and that they would take care of you whenever you get sick, rather than go to a nursing home."

"Yep, that's right," Bill replied with a grin. "That's how I want it to work out."

And so it did. When Bill's health began to slide, he moved in with the pastor. Home health-care workers stopped by every few days, but the main responsibility lay with John and Linda. On Bill's last night on earth, they played gospel music for him and a sermon by COGIC Presiding Bishop Charles E. Blake. By the next morning, the old gentleman had gone to be with the Lord.

"He died a happy man," John says. "And when his will was probated, sure enough—he had willed the house to us. I looked at my wife and said, 'So *this* is what the Spirit told us that day back in Virginia. Praise the Lord!'"

The Pentons still live in their "gift house" as they lead a thriving Tacoma church, called Greater Heights Church of God in Christ. They give ongoing thanks for the favor of God, who turned their financial crisis into blessing so they could continue serving him with unburdened hearts.

chapter 26

A MIRACLE
FOR MOM

In 2010, when the Avilán family of four arrived in Vancouver from their native Venezuela, they faced the challenges all immigrants face: finding employment, learning a new language, and figuring out a different culture. Three years later, they certainly didn't need the additional stress that came when Doris, the forty-six-year-old mother, was diagnosed with a five-centimeter (two-inch) tumor in her colon.

This diagnosis immediately revived memories of the woman's sister and aunt, both of whom had died from colon cancer. "It was very hard on all of us," says her young-adult daughter, Dorielis (Dori). "It would have been even harder if our family had not just come to know the Lord through the ministry of Coastal Church. My father, who had always claimed to be an agnostic, had been invited by a friend to try the Alpha course that the church offered. By the end of the course, he had been touched by the Holy Spirit and had asked Jesus into his heart. The same thing happened to me the next time Alpha was offered. Then, my younger brother came to the Lord, and finally, my mom."

But in the face of this serious health threat, the family's prayers turned more toward the vein of *Oh, God—we just started following you. And now this!* Their confidence in a loving and caring God was definitely jostled.

The mother quickly underwent surgery at the world-class St. Paul's Hospital in downtown Vancouver, with the forecast that chemotherapy would need to follow once she recovered. Dori quit her job as a travel agent in order to be at her mother's bedside as much as possible. "A pastor from the church had given me a Spanish Bible, which I read to her there in the hospital. People stopped by to pray for her, which built up our faith somewhat."

But over the course of the post-surgical month, the mom steadily grew weaker, not better. She was losing blood, she threw up anything she tried to eat, her weight kept slipping, and she hardly opened her eyes. A ventilator was needed to help her breathe, and a feeding tube down her throat provided her only nutrition.

Eventually, the attending doctor came to an alarming conclusion. "It looks like we're going to have to do another surgery," he announced. "There must be something else in there that we didn't see the first time."

Dori was genuinely frightened. She doubted whether her mother would survive a second trip to the operation room. If she didn't make it, how would the rest of the family carry on in this new land without her?

"I retreated that morning to the visitors' lounge on the tenth floor and began crying out to the Lord," she recalls. "The place happened to be empty except for me, and so I felt free to say, 'God, you just can't let her die. Please heal my mom! If you do, I promise I'll tell everyone about it!'"

In that moment, as she looked out across the Vancouver skyline, a vision came before her eyes. She saw the figure of Jesus standing atop one of the buildings. Light came from his hands, streaming down toward the street as well as up toward the sky. Dori seemed to hear him say, *I have been given authority in heaven and on earth to heal your mom—and I will do so!*

Swept up with both joy and peace, she quickly returned to tell her mother what had just happened. A tear began coursing down the mother's cheek. By the time Dori finished her account, she was so relieved that she leaned across onto her mother's lap and fell asleep.

Fifteen minutes later, she felt a tapping on her head. "Dori, wake up," the mother said—the first words she had attempted in many days. "Please call the nurse. I need this tube taken out of my throat! I'm hungry!"

Amazed, Dori called the nurse, who did as the patient requested. Food was brought, and the mother ate successfully for the first time in weeks.

Not long afterward, she had a new idea. "I just want to go for a walk," she said. She got out of bed under her own power. Moving steadily down the hospital corridor, she added, "Dori, while you were napping, I had a vision of heaven. I saw people there whom I knew in the past! And they were saying goodbye to me—that I wasn't going to be there with all of them just yet.

"Then as soon as the vision went away, I felt completely well. That's when I woke you up.

"Now I need for you to call the doctor and tell him in English all about this. I want to get tested again and see if I can go home!"

When the physician arrived in her room, he was understandably surprised. "Well, you certainly look much stronger," he said. "Let's run some tests and see what we learn."

Within hours, the results came back: the cancer was gone! She was discharged, and by that very evening, mother and daughter were *walking* back to their home three blocks away.

"Don't you want to take a taxi?" Dori asked.

"No," came the reply. "I've been in bed for so long. Now I have the energy to walk, so I want to do it!"

Today, approaching the five-year mark, Doris Avilán remains in excellent health. She doesn't get to see her daughter as often now, since the young woman's marriage in 2016 and relocation to Manitoba. But the two women will never forget that day when the Great Physician showed up in dramatic fashion. They are more than excited to tell the story again and again to all who will listen.

chapter 27

SHOWDOWN AT THE ALTAR

People responding to a public altar call for salvation are usually quiet, moving forward with measured steps and downcast eyes—but not this man.

On the fourth night of a weeklong revival meeting at Mount Zion Holiness Church of God in Galax, Virginia, the stocky man of medium height in his late thirties was about halfway down the center aisle when he suddenly burst out, "HELP ME! HELP ME!" The startled 250 or so worshipers in the pews shuddered, wondering what would happen next.

"I looked at his face," says Bishop Harry Cohen, the guest evangelist who was conducting the meeting, "and it seemed contorted. I discerned that he had some kind of demon possession, and so I asked for the church elders and visiting ministers to accompany me.

"As the man reached the front, we formed a circle around him. We were close enough to tell he'd been drinking. In that moment, I felt led to give explicit instruction that none of the other ministers should actually touch him, because we were dealing with a powerful spirit here. I also said to the congregation, 'Everyone here tonight, please go to prayer.'

"The man's twisted facial features sent chills over my body. I admit, I was initially a bit fearful of what we were getting into. But then the Holy Spirit calmed me, assuring me he would be in control."

The bishop began to lay his hands on the man and call out the spirit from within him. Just then, however, an additional minister broke into the circle and laid his hands on the man, contrary to the instruction. He tried to rebuke the spirit. The troubled man violently pushed him backward and exclaimed in an eerie, almost split-pitched (both high and low at the same time) voice, "I'm not coming out, because you have no power!"

Was Satan going to win this face-off after all?

Before the meeting dissolved into chaos, Bishop Cohen laid hands on him once again and spoke with authority: "Holy Spirit, *you* take control of this fellow. This demon from hell has come to strip him of all his mental faculties. Pull it out of him, and send it into oblivion!"

The man crumpled to the floor, tossed and turned for a moment, and then went totally limp for several minutes. When he finally opened his eyes, he was crying and softly repeating, "Thank God, thank God." The entire church broke into rejoicing.

Helping him up from the floor, Bishop Cohen asked, "How do you feel now?"

"I feel like something has been lifted off of me," he replied as the tears continued to flow. "I'm free! I'm free!"

The local pastor had never seen this man before and knew nothing of his history, but was, of course, glad for his deliverance. The revival services had been widely publicized, and perhaps that is what drew him to attend that particular night, seeking help.

The best part of the story is that this troubled man, once set free, "ended up being a preacher in South Carolina," Harry Cohen reports. The two of them got back in touch by phone just a few years ago.

Cohen, now the general president and presiding bishop of the United Holy Church of America, says, "Satan is a liar from the pit. Sometimes we fail to allow the all-powerful Spirit to direct us in confronting the Evil One and casting him out. If we don't let the Spirit lead the way, 'self' will make a big mess of things. It's far better to use divine power to overcome the works of the Devil."

chapter 28

JUST TAKING A WALK

Some readers today may find it hard to believe that budding preachers were once given pulpit opportunities before they were even old enough to vote or serve in the military. Robert Fort, now the seasoned chairman of the United Evangelical Churches (UEC), still remembers a certain Friday night during a weeklong series of revival meetings that he, though only seventeen years old, was conducting in the small farming town of Shafter, California. It turned into something more unique than anyone would have imagined. He tells the story:

We had begun the meeting on a Sunday morning, and I soon noticed a certain severely disabled man who sat with his wife in the second row at every service. She helped him "walk" by steadying him on his left side while he used a wooden cane in his right hand. With the cane's help, he would lean on his right leg while swinging his left side and leg forward, his wife holding tightly to his arm. Then, he would hobble a few inches forward on his right leg in a slight jumping motion before starting the process all over. It was painful even to watch.

But at least he was able to avoid using a wheelchair and maintain some degree of personal mobility.

After the service on Monday evening, he told me he had made history in medical journals as the patient who had survived the largest brain tumor removal (at that time) and still be "left with any sense" (his words). This daring surgery had happened sixteen years before, leaving him paralyzed on his left side, from his head and face down to his toes. Doctors had told him he would never walk again and that he should "be happy you can still think clearly."

His speech was somewhat slurred by the impairment to the left side of his face. However, through much perseverance and with assistance from his faithful wife, he had learned to speak fairly understandably and to "walk" in the manner I witnessed.

High Drama at the Altar

The two of them attended every service that week. Finally, on Friday evening, I sensed that God wanted to touch him.

I spoke to him as he sat in the second row and said, "Brother, this is your night." I asked him to come to the altar area of the church. This he did, slowly and laboriously, until at last he stood before me—the cane in his right hand, and his wife holding his left arm.

I motioned toward the cane and asked him a question I have never asked anyone before or since. "Would you mind if I broke that?"

"You can if you want," he simply replied.

So with permission granted, I carefully took the cane from his right hand, leaving him to balance himself precariously on his right leg and his wife's arm. I then snapped it in half over my knee. As I turned away to toss the two pieces toward the empty platform behind me, I remember being surprised that it had broken so easily.

I then turned back toward the man and his wife, thinking I would now lay my hands on him and ask God to heal him.

But to my amazement, the miracle had already begun. The fingers on his left hand were twitching, and his wife was staring at them with her mouth wide open. Then, his left hand began to move ... then his arm and shoulder ... then his face began to vibrate and tremble as the muscles and nerves came back to life.

By this time, he was crying and saying, "Thank you, Jesus! Thank you, God!" He raised his left leg several times, bending it at the knee. His wife let out a scream I will never forget. By this time, the whole congregation and I were crying.

I still had not touched him or even prayed for him. He kept raising his leg and moving his arm up and down two or three times. Then, he took off running around the church. People were shouting, clapping, rejoicing, and praising God all over the building. His wife was weeping, her hands raised toward heaven. I was transfixed in awe at the miracle taking place right before my eyes.

I don't remember anything else about that service. We had all witnessed sixteen years of paralysis reversed in a moment of time by the mercy and power of the living God.

What I do remember clearly was that the next night's service (Saturday evening) was so packed with people ahead of starting time that the little Assembly of God sanctuary could not contain them. There wasn't even standing room. We had to move the PA speakers and aim them out the windows so those standing outside or sitting in cars in the parking lot could hear the message.

I went down to hug the brother who had been healed the night before. "Where did all these people come from?" I asked.

He replied, "Oh, I just took a walk downtown today."

chapter 29

TIME TO UPROOT

Chris and Carol Ball had been married just a year when they came to the quiet hamlet of South Butler, New York (population 127), in a farming area between Lake Ontario and the Finger Lakes. There they found themselves cocooned in tradition and stability. The denominational church they would pastor had been founded long ago, in 1831. Sunday morning attendance now ran in the low thirties.

The couple settled in for the long haul, giving themselves over to meeting and loving the people. Their ministry was welcomed, and in time, the church began to grow. "I led the congregation gradually," says Pastor Chris, "to embrace the concept of a church being 'built on the foundation of the apostles and prophets, with Christ Jesus himself as the chief cornerstone.'[1] I taught about the precedents of the New Testament church and how they set a pattern for us today."

In time, he invited an elderly Welsh minister named Stanley Hammond, who had impressed him during his student days at Elim Bible Institute (Lima, NY), to come teach about the gifts of the Spirit. This dignified, gentle guest had told about his first experience as a teenager in the Apostolic Church of Wales, when after giving a prophetic word in the congregation, his pastor had

called him in. Hammond expected to be congratulated for what had occurred. Instead, the pastor said, "Stanley, it's very clear that you have a word from God. But I want to tell you what you need to do now." Holding up a Bible, he continued, "You need to eat, drink, and sleep this book so that what comes out of your mouth agrees with what it says here."

Says Pastor Chris, "This was exactly the kind of grounded, trustworthy model I wanted to put before our people. And they accepted it."

Later, when the pastor began looking for additional property to accommodate the church's growth, he ran into resistance; land-owners in this area just *did not* part with what had been in their family for generations. More than once he approached the adjacent farmer, trying to buy ten acres, and got turned down. The man had agreed to let the church put a gravel parking lot on a small corner of his space, but that was as far as he would go.

Then, a visiting minister from Pennsylvania, named Dennis Cramer, came to conduct a training weekend on prophecy, continuing in the same vein as Stanley Hammond. He was tall, articulate, with glasses and graying hair—the kind of spokesman for the supernatural who made people feel comfortable.

Between sessions, Cramer said to the pastor, "I somehow think that God really wants to bless this church with greater facilities." Pastor Ball explained the limitations. But after returning home, the speaker called back the following Tuesday to press the issue, saying he was going to return a portion of his honorarium. "Take this money to the farmer once again," he instructed. "You're not asking for enough land!"

Chris thought this was pointless, but he did as requested. Entering the neighboring man's home once again, he took a deep breath and ventured a bold opening line. "Here is a check for $1,000," he said. "Are you sure you don't want to sell us anything?"

The farmer thought for a moment, then shocked him by replying, "Well ... would you take forty acres?"

"Absolutely!" Pastor Ball replied. The men agreed on a fair price, shook hands, and the deal was set. The church (which by now had affiliated with the Elim group) would be able to expand after all, thanks to a prophet's challenge.

A Bold Word

Every two or three years thereafter, Dennis Cramer was invited to return to the small New York village for more teaching. Both the pastor and congregation trusted his use of the prophetic word. When he gave inspired messages for the church as a whole (in contrast to individuals), they transcribed the words onto a prayer wall, asking God what they should do practically, to allow the prophecy to come to pass.

Over the years, the pastoral couple became firmly planted in this part of God's vineyard; three children were born along the way and grew up in the loving environment. The church changed its name to Lighthouse Community Fellowship. Chris took on a few outside involvements—becoming the part-time general secretary of Elim Fellowship, for one—but his heart remained anchored in South Butler. At an elders' retreat in January 2014, he said, "I know Carol and I have been here twenty-six years now, but I feel as though I've got another good ten years left. I want you to know that I'm not intending to go anywhere else. I'm here to stay."

But the very next month, Elim Fellowship President Ron Burgio called Chris to say his season at this leadership post was done, and Chris should become his successor, if the group's Council of Elders would agree. The pastor listened politely but immediately began thinking of how much he loved pastoring. He looked around at the spacious buildings that had been erected debt-free, some $3 million worth. The congregation was healthy, now some 450 strong—in a village hardly a fourth as large.

Should he and his wife uproot from all this and move an hour west to the fellowship headquarters in Lima? How hard it would be to say goodbye to cherished longtime friends!

"I was not sure what to make of this overture," he says, "and when I brought it up with my wife, she was understandably hesitant. The entire life she had built for us here was at risk. We agreed to just pray about it and otherwise keep quiet, for obvious reasons."

The month of March brought another of the periodic Dennis Cramer visits. By now, he had become a familiar face to the Balls and the congregation. On the very first evening, he boldly called Chris and Carol forward to the podium, where he laid his hands on their heads and began to prophesy—in front of the entire church:

Promotion! Promotion! Promotion! Promotion! You have thought that this church was the end of the line for your ministry. But it is not.

I, the Lord, brought you here, and you have done well. But now a change is about to come—in the next two to three years. You need to get ready, because I want you to minister more broadly to the churches across the Elim Fellowship.

I will use you both in this new role. Chris, you will be a man who leads from your heart; do not compromise that. Carol, you will see new ministry in prophetic ways. This is the word for you both tonight.

How had he known?! There was no earthly way. Under normal circumstances, the Balls would have been upset to have such a word given in public. But they could hardly deny its authenticity, given the recent call about the presidency. Dennis Cramer had no inside scoop—but God did.

The elders and others in the congregation were not entirely shocked, having noticed the wider impact of their longtime pastor's ministry. They gave their affirmation to this new opening. Lighthouse's young associate pastor and his wife, whom Chris and Carol Ball had mentored extensively, would make a worthy replacement to lead the church forward.

The Elim nomination and interview process got underway, and in due time, the name of Chris Ball was confirmed to lead Elim Fellowship's work across not only the American churches (mainly in the Northeast) but on mission fields across the globe. He is now focused on equipping the next generation of leaders to advance the fellowship's contribution to the kingdom of God.

Looking back on this transition, he is level-headed. "I'm not one to *live* by the prophetic," he says. "I see these words more as a confirmation of what God is leading to be done. Yes, there's a directive element. But the Lord has many ways to make his will known. Our churches readily embrace the gift of prophecy, along with the other gifts. They are a meaningful and important component of New Testament Christianity."

"WAKE UP, *MIJA!*"

Every delivery room has its moments of drama. But few could match what took place at Hemet Valley Medical Center (Southern California), in late 2006, when a baby girl emerged after a long labor with the umbilical cord tightly wrapped around her neck. The family's pastor, Peter Edwards of New Life Open Bible Church in San Jacinto, tells the story:

Manuel and Maria Hernandez, a couple at our church, were happily married and raising three teenagers when, unexpectedly, Maria became pregnant.

It had been fourteen years since their last child, Cherissa, had been born. The couple had suffered a miscarriage just a year before, due to Maria's diabetes. But now, they embraced this new pregnancy as it proceeded to full term.

In the early hours of November 27, Maria went into labor. They arrived at the hospital at approximately 4:45 a.m. The morning passed slowly, then midday, and the longer things dragged on, the more apparent it became that both mom and baby were having trouble. Manuel and his daughter saw concerned looks in the eyes of the doctor and nurses, so they began to pray. "I didn't want to alarm Maria," he says. "We just started worshiping our Lord. Since God inhabits our praises,[1] I knew he would be with us."

At last, after much struggle, a nine-pound two-ounce girl—Siara Monique—was born at 2:38 p.m. Manuel quickly noticed the cord tangled around her neck, and her skin was blue.

A Code Blue had already gone out while Siara was still in the birth canal, summoning a "crash team"—an ER doctor, a pediatrician, an ER nurse, a respiratory therapist, among others. Now they immediately went to work. They quickly took the APGAR ratings—**A**ppearance (skin color), **P**ulse rate, **G**rimace (response to stimulation), **A**ctivity, and **R**espiration (breathing, crying). The maximum possible score is 10 (two points for each category). Siara got a total of zero.

"As the doctors and nurses were putting their training and experience to work in the fight for our daughter's survival," Manuel says, "so were we. Maria, Cherissa, and I all prayed in the Spirit, trusting God for his perfect will. We declared the Devil a liar and spoke life to Siara."

Manuel also quickly phoned his son, Manuel III, and asked him to pray, knowing he would call others. People across the country quickly went to God on behalf of Siara.

No Response

The team kept working for five full minutes … ten minutes … fifteen minutes. Finally, after an agonizing twenty-one minutes of heroic effort, Siara was officially pronounced dead, and a death certificate was signed. Nurses wept as they left the delivery room.

Manuel, however, was not about to concede defeat. "I felt impressed by the Lord to walk over to the baby, slowly, so as not to alarm the medical personnel. I thought, *God, you have never failed me, and I know you won't start now.*

Manuel put his hands over his lifeless child and reminded God that the breath of life comes from him. He prayed in tongues; he prayed in English while the medical staff waited respectfully. (The

ER nurse mistakenly assumed he was Native American and later said, "He prayed the most beautiful prayer in an Indian dialect!")

At one point, Manuel declared with boldness, "God, so that everyone here will know you are alive and love your children, I say, 'Siara, come forth!'"

Eventually, the respiratory therapist stepped in and said quietly, "Let's take her to Mommy," intending to allow the mother to grieve. She wrapped the limp body in a blanket and carried her to Maria, who cradled the infant in her arms. But she, like her husband, was not ready to surrender. She reminded her that she had been moving in her womb a short time before. "Come on, *mija,*" (my daughter)—"wake up!" she pleaded.

. . . And Then

The baby's skin color remained purplish, but suddenly, Maria noticed her chest moving. "Come look at this!" Maria called to the medical staff.

"It's just the oxygen from our attempts to revive her that is now being expelled," the respiratory therapist explained.

As Maria tells the story today, she testifies that at that moment, she could hear my wife, Starla, say (paraphrasing the words of Psalm 118:17), "She shall not die, but shall live and declare the glory of God!" Maria felt she had a choice to make. She could accept what the technician was saying, or she could keep believing God.

The doctor, hoping to comfort the distraught mother, embraced Mom and baby. And then, "I feel something!" he exclaimed. Calling for a pediatric stethoscope, he listened to Siara's chest. "I've got a heartbeat!" he called out.

He carried Siara into the adjacent room where the "crash team" was debriefing and exclaimed, "I've got a pulse!" It was at this point that I arrived in the maternity ward. As soon as I identified myself, they rushed me into the room where Siara was lying in an incubator with the team standing all around, discussing what they should do. Their dilemma was whether to exercise "mercy" by doing nothing and thereby allowing Siara to pass away or to try to revive her, virtually guaranteeing that the Hernandez family would face the burden of caring for a severely brain-damaged child.

They politely stepped aside to allow me to lay hands on Siara and pray. Her skin color was still a ghastly purple, although there was a small pink area on her chest.

At the end of my prayer, I joined the parents, who were still in the delivery room, where we continued to pray and worship. Soon, the head of nursing services began shuttling back and forth, encouraging us to continue praying as she gave us updates. She showed her spiritual understanding when she said to us, "If God could raise old stinky Lazarus, he can raise this baby!" Manuel and Maria were enveloped in an amazing peace. The presence of God in that delivery room was unlike anything I have ever experienced.

Siara was soon airlifted over the hills to the world-famous NICU (neonatal intensive-care unit) at Loma Linda University Children's Hospital for monitoring. All the experts were sure that she would need a lot of care after such a traumatic birth. She suffered a few seizures at first, but soon they stopped. The staff began referring to her as "Baby Lazarus."

And on December 8, little eleven-day-old Siara came home to stay. Today, she is a normal, active ten-year-old in our church.

In the words of the ER nurse who was present that day, "Siara Monique Hernandez was not revived. She was resurrected."

THE SPIRITUAL
ROOKIE

For everyone who assumes that spiritual gifts function only through seasoned saints, after a lengthy apprenticeship in the Christian walk, consider the case of a Middle Eastern immigrant to Florida named Ali.

After more than two decades in the Tampa area, his English is now solid, and he works hard as a cook for Village Inn—in fact, pulling double shifts at two different restaurants (one morning, the other evening)—to support his wife and two daughters. The older daughter is a student at Florida State while the younger one is just finishing high school.

Ali's spiritual quest was triggered when his daughters kept badgering him to come to church with them. He kept resisting, while privately asking himself, *So who is God? Is Jesus real?* Not long afterward, he had an unusual dream in which oversized hands descended from the sky, cupping a globe. A steady flow of breath seemed to make the globe spin. What was this supposed to mean? He didn't know.

He told the story at work; however, his fellow employees had few answers. Then one day, Pastor Don Evans and his wife came in to have lunch with a church family. Their waitress, overhearing their conversation, asked as the meal was concluding, "I was just wondering—are you a minister?"

"Yes, I am," he replied.

"There's someone here in the kitchen who needs to talk to a minister. Would you be willing to speak with him?"

The pastor nodded yes. "Will he come here to the table?"

"No," she answered. "He's in work clothes. I'll find a better place for you to talk."

Escorting him back to an alcove off the kitchen area, she soon introduced him to a man in a cook's apron, wearing clog shoes and a baseball cap turned backward. The pastor extended his hand and said, "So your name is Ali?"

"Yes, I'm Ali—and I've been a Muslim. But, I have experienced something of Jesus Christ, and I need a mentor to help me understand what's happening."

This clearly wasn't the time or place for an extended conversation, so the two arranged to meet the next Tuesday, which was Ali's only day off. He would come to the pastor's office at Gateway Christian Center.

After being welcomed and seated, Ali told the pastor about the dream of the globe that spun. "What did that mean?" he wanted to know.

"Well, let's talk about the imagery," Pastor Evans replied. "The heavens … hands much bigger than the world itself … and some kind of breath making the world rotate. I think God was showing you who's actually in control. After all, couldn't those hands have just closed down on that globe and stopped its motion? Or even crushed it?"

At this, Ali began to tear up. "I never analyzed the dream, but I just accepted that it was from God," he said. "But *what* God? Was it Allah? Or Jesus?"

"Let me mention something from the story of Christ," the pastor replied. "When he was crucified, the soldiers pierced his hands with nails. In your dream, did you see any scars or wounds on those hands?"

Ali thought for a moment. "Now that you mention it … yes."

"Then that would seem to indicate that this was Jesus, answering your call for insight."

A Second Image

Soon Ali was telling about another experience that happened not while he was asleep, but in real time. "I was out on a boat in the Gulf, still thinking about what the dream had meant. I said that day, *God, I need a sign of some kind. What kind of sign could you give me?*

"Before I got back to the dock, the clouds parted, and there was a rainbow! It was beautiful.

"I went back to work the next day and told people what had happened. Somebody in the kitchen said, 'Well, in the Bible God gave the rainbow as the sign of a promise.' I had been asking for a sign, so maybe it was. What do you think, Pastor?"

"The Bible has many, many promises God has made," the pastor replied. "The rainbow was a unique moment in history, after God had sent judgment on the earth by means of a flood. He had seen people so wicked that there was no hope to redeem the situation without eliminating them and starting over. You may have heard, though, that he chose one family to repopulate the earth."

That triggered a question: "Would the Lord ever flood the earth again?" he asked. "People today are very wicked."

"No—that's what the rainbow meant. It was God's promise that this would never be repeated. But his greatest sign was to send Jesus Christ onto the earth in a miraculous way." Pastor Evans then proceeded to describe the immaculate conception of

Jesus; how he was born and grew up living a sinless life; how he began ministering at the age of thirty; and how people realized he was not a mortal man but had been sent by God.

At this point, Ali interjected, "Most Muslims keep asking themselves, if God is almighty, why did he need a son to die?"

"That's a deep question," the pastor answered, "with a lot of background in Old Testament history. But I will give you a simple answer. God *didn't* need a son to die. But *I* needed someone human who could prove to me that I could live a higher kind of life, through his grace and mercy. God sent his son to die so that all humans could understand—though we are all guilty before God, he can set us free. That includes you, Ali."

The man began to weep, covering his face with his hands. In a few moments, the pastor continued, "Ali, I think you've already experienced the presence of God in your searching. But there's an act of surrender at which point you give him who you are."

"I'm nobody special," he answered. "What does someone like me have to give to God?"

"The rest of your *life.*"

Soon the pastor led in prayer, and then Ali prayed aloud. It was a moment of crossing over into the grace and forgiveness of Christ.

At the end of the session, Ali said, "I want to keep talking with you, if I may. When I was wondering about all these things, it seemed like God said to me, *I will send someone to you. You will know that he is from me.* And now I see that you're the one!"

"Sure, we can keep meeting," the pastor answered. This turned out to be the first of many Tuesday appointments.

Empowered to Witness

From that point on, Ali began willingly going to church with his girls on Saturday night, ahead of his Sunday work schedules.

During one worship time, he voluntarily lifted his hands in praise to the Lord. Suddenly, without any prior instruction or exposure, he began speaking in an unknown language.

He called Pastor Evans immediately after. "We have to talk!"

"Okay. Can it wait until Tuesday?"

"No! Something has happened that I don't understand."

"Okay. I'll come to the restaurant tomorrow after my service ends."

The pastor feared that there had been some crisis of faith. He was pleasantly surprised to hear Ali say, "Everyone was singing, and the words were right there on the screen. But I started saying things that weren't written there! I know my native Arabic tongue, I know English—but this was neither one. What happened to me?"

The pastor opened his Bible to teach from Acts chapter 2. "Back when you first came to my office, you surrendered to the will of God. And now, he has filled you with his Holy Spirit to be a witness for him."

Ali took this literally; he began talking about Jesus with nearly anyone he met. He almost expected that every time he shared the Good News, people would just melt and receive Christ. It didn't always happen that way, of course. In time, his boss reprimanded him for talking about "religion" with customers. He was told to stay in the kitchen, no matter if he sensed a need in someone outside.

However, this still allowed him to witness to the waitresses. They were intrigued that he had suddenly dropped his long-ingrained habit of smoking. They asked interesting questions. Some of the women, however, brushed him aside, rudely.

Ali expressed his disappointment about these rebuffs to Pastor Evans. The pastor answered, "Well, you know very well from your past how militant Islam often beats people into submission.

But now, you have to trust that God knows the perfect time and place for each person either to accept or deny the gospel. Everyone comes to a crossroads sooner or later. And some choose the wrong way. You're responsible only to share the truth—preferably through your own testimony. When you say that you used to be a Muslim, and then God picked you to undergo a radical change, it will go much better."

Together they explored the Parable of the Sower, in which some seed fell on hard ground or among thorns, producing no results. But other seed fell on good, receptive soil. "You never know how your witness will be received," the pastor said. "That's okay—just keep sowing the seed."

Supernatural Gifting

The intriguing part of the Ali story is that the gifts of the Spirit were not delayed in this young believer's life. Though only a Christ-follower for a matter of months, he began seeing the Lord work through him to bring new life and understanding in multiple settings.

One of the waitresses, expecting a child, was crying at work because of troubling physical symptoms. She had already miscarried once before, and now she feared another disappointment would strike.

Ali said, "Would you let me pray for you?"

"Yes," she answered.

He began to pray right there in the kitchen: "God, please give my friend peace, and help her to trust you that this baby will be born safely and will become a child of God."

The symptoms cleared up, and in time she delivered a healthy child.

On another occasion, he said to the boss who had curbed his enthusiasm for witnessing, "You seem different today. But God told me to tell you that the things that look so bad right now will be cleared up in three days!"

"Look, Ali," she said with a scowl, "I'm telling you again—keep your God to yourself! You're getting out of hand with this."

"I'm sorry," Ali replied. "But I really did hear him say that, and he told me to tell you."

"Well," she snapped, "just fix the eggs and pancakes, will you?"

Three days later, however, she came back to apologize with tears in her eyes. "You would not have known, but there was a problem with our audit here—the numbers were off, and I couldn't figure out why. I could have lost my job over this. But they found the error, and everything balanced out after all."

It has gotten to the point that Pastor Evans opens nearly every Tuesday session by saying, "Okay, Ali—what happened this week?! Fill me in on the latest thing God is doing through you."

The work of the Spirit through a willing and open vessel is not as complicated as many have thought. It is entirely normal in the flow of Spirit-filled living.

chapter 32

NOT TOO COLD TO BELIEVE

If you think the winters in Montreal are long, cold, and dark, try living another thousand miles north in the Inuit town of Kangirsuk. The average *high* temperature in February is -19 degrees Celsius (-2 degrees Fahrenheit), while the average overnight *low* is -27 C. (-16 F.). Heating oil for the entire community (594 souls) arrives once a year by ship, when the ice on Ungava Bay gives way between July and September. Otherwise, there is no firewood to burn, as the town sits well north of the Arctic tree line.

Elizabeth Annahatak grew up in this town, moved away for fifteen years, began working in youth ministry, and then sensed a call to return home. At the small Kangirsuk Full Gospel Church, she quickly volunteered to help lead worship and work with young people; before long, she was even preaching and serving on the eldership board as treasurer.

The elderly pastor, Peter Niqi Airo, would say to the young woman from time to time, "We really need to find a way to build a better building. Several years ago we had plans drawn up by an architect, but how would we ever raise the money?"—an estimated half-million dollars.

The problems of the aging structure were obvious: it seated fewer than forty people; it didn't comply with numerous building codes; it had no restrooms; there was evidence of mold throughout; black flies found their way indoors every spring and summer; and the shaky electrical wiring couldn't simultaneously keep up with both the sound equipment at the front and the coffee maker in the back. Plus, the insulation was no match for the icy winter blasts.

To build something new, however, would require a major amount of faith. All the lumber, sheetrock, doors, and other materials would have to be brought in by ship from the south. They certainly wouldn't fit in the cargo bays of the small Air Inuit planes (Dash 8 turboprops) that landed once (or at the most, twice) a day, nor could the astronomical freight charges be absorbed. And there were no roads into the town from any direction—nor any Home Depots or Lowe's stores waiting on the other end.

A Humble Beginning

Not knowing what a master strategy would even look like, Elizabeth and her fellow believers felt led to make a start anyway. Their beloved pastor died of cancer in September 2010, but his vision lived on as Elizabeth eventually succeeded him.

"We had around $50,000 saved up, and we had a plot of ground," she says. "So we started fund-raising—making colorful hats and warm boots to sell, holding bake sales and garage sales, even picking up pop cans to recycle. I sent letters to other churches I knew, both here in the north and down south, asking for support.

"I'd also had a little experience in the political realm, enough to know about some government programs and Inuit development organizations that might consider us, as a form of community advancement. Some of them responded with modest grants. Each year, our building fund made a little more progress. We knew we couldn't build all at once; we'd have to take things in stages.

"But we just kept praying for the Lord to provide."

By 2014, she had gained the counsel of Rev. David Ellyatt in southern Ontario, who is the director of Arctic Missions Outreach Trust Fund,[1] which focuses on sending construction teams to build churches across Canada's Far North. This mission had helped the Kangirsuk church over the years, and now it arranged for them to get their blueprints redrawn so the Province of Quebec would approve them, which resulted in a more realistic cost estimate: a million dollars. For a 3,300-square-foot building, that may sound high to contractors in more temperate zones, but it is entirely understandable when dealing with permafrost, long supply lines, and other challenges. For example, the ceiling and underfloor insulation alone would need to be R-64, more than twice the protection of an average building in the United States.

Rev. Ellyatt guided Elizabeth in finding discounts on everything from ductwork to airfares. The goal: a modern, attractive church with a spacious worship center, a multipurpose room, a kitchenette, restrooms, office space, storage—all in all, four times the size of the old building.

Teams began arriving that summer, using as much material as the church had been able to order. Bit by bit, the building began to take shape. "Our goal was to finish the outside of the building before winter arrived," Elizabeth says. "However, even in December another team came, in spite of the snow and cold."

Momentum

Progress picked up speed again when the summer of 2015 arrived. By then, more funding had made possible the purchase of another shipment of everything from windows to carpeting. "We marveled at how these men would leave their homes for two or even three weeks at a time to come up and help us," she says with joy. "We arranged for them to stay in homes and tried to feed them generously as they worked hard six days a week, ten hours a day. I'd never seen anything like this. It brought tears to my eyes.

"The Lord kept putting various experts in my path as I needed them—for example, at one point we needed a certain kind of saw to cut the exterior siding. A source showed up for that. The plumbing and electrical work had to be done by local men with certification, and again the hand of the Lord provided. He kept sending what we needed, both in skills and in money—it was crazy!"

They always found enough homes to host the workers, so as not to have to spend $150 or more a night per room at the small local hotel. They managed to acquire a used SUV for a bargain price to haul men and materials back and forth. One wife of a construction volunteer was so moved that she came up for the entire summer to cook for the teams.

Interior plastering began in October, using church volunteers alongside the teams. Flooring followed in November, and by December, the power could be turned on.

"Near the end, the Lord even sent a woman from another community to come and help clean the floors and move in our chairs," Elizabeth says. "She told us that while praying that morning, she had heard the Lord tell her to come and help. We cried in awe that God would send someone from a different place to help us move in!"

Services began in the new building in January 2016. For the formal dedication weekend in late May, David Ellyatt flew up along with Paul McPhail, general secretary of the Independent Assemblies of God International (Canada), to honor and celebrate this accomplishment. "This congregation had moved into their building debt-free!" says Ellyatt. "And they had raised perhaps 95

MIRACLE INVASION

percent of the money themselves, which is remarkable, especially given the area's low employment. Our mission just basically provided the volunteer work teams."

When Elizabeth Annahatak looks back, she reflects, "It was too big a task, too heavy to think more than a day ahead at a time. But God was faithful; he brought his favor throughout the entire process. When we felt we could not move forward, the gift of faith still kept coming, bringing with it encouragement and promises."

When she stands before her congregation week after week, or leads the youth study on cold nights, she can hardly contain her joy. Young mothers don't have to worry about their little ones crawling on the floor anymore. People with respiratory issues are no longer at risk. Brunches and other food events are now possible.

The church has even played host to regional conferences of Inuit churches. One marriage conference drew especially strong attendance, with people flying in from other settlements. And, an area training program for youth discipleship is on the drawing boards. "It's so exciting!" the young pastor says. "Now that the building is up, we're focusing on building people up. We don't just have to purchase nails anymore; we can help raise up the kingdom of God here in the north."

To see an inspiring slide show of the Kangirsuk project, go to: www.goo.gl/unXvvu.

chapter 33

HEARTBREAK, THEN HEALING

This account, by Pastor Steve Gardner (Christ the Rock Church of God, Knoxville, Tennessee), starts out with perhaps the saddest words an eager young couple will ever hear:

Y ou will never be able to have children."

For two people who loved kids, that news was devastating to my wife and me. I remember the empty, surreal feeling that filled our souls as we contemplated life without children. We were heartbroken, and shared the dreadful news with our family and closest friends only.

Shortly thereafter, a pastor friend called to tell us about a young woman in his church who was pregnant and wanted to place her baby with a good Christian couple. He told her about us, and soon we were on our way to meet her. Our sadness was turning a corner—or so we thought.

We met her, and she proceeded to "choose" us as her baby's adoptive parents. We were thrilled. We soon found out she was carrying a little boy and began making arrangements to receive him into our lives. I remember sitting in a restaurant and giddily talking with my wife about all we needed to get "our son." My list included a baseball glove and a Bible!

163

The day of his delivery came, and we were there at the hospital to pray with the birth mother. He was born, and the hospital hosted a "parents' dinner" for us.

However, within a few days, his birth mother changed her mind, deciding to keep the baby.

Again, devastation and heartache flooded our souls like polluted water. Was this some kind of cruel joke? Were we destined to be childless? Were we suffering for some past sin?

So many questions crowded our minds, and it was difficult to hear the voice of the Lord. The weeks that followed that devastating experience were filled with a bevy of emotions. We went through our daily routines on autopilot.

We pastor a church, so we had people who needed us. But how could we talk about faith and purpose when our own faith was riddled with hurts that only parents who have lost children can understand?

Not the End of the Story

God was gracious during this time, and Isaiah 55:8–9 became real for us. It reads:

"For my thoughts are not your thoughts,
neither are your ways my ways,"
declares the LORD.
"As the heavens are higher than the earth,
so are my ways higher than your ways
and my thoughts than your thoughts."

However, it wasn't until eight years later that we understood how much "higher" God's ways were above ours. One day, my wife got a call from someone she had not heard from in eight years—the birth mother of the boy we had planned to adopt.

She was crying as she explained to us that her son had been in a horrible bicycle accident. While riding down a hill, he had flipped his bike. The kickstand had actually penetrated his eye and lodged in his brain. He was now in a coma in the ICU, and his head had swollen to a huge degree.

She told us the doctors had said if he lived, he would have severe brain damage. Then she asked if we would make the three-hour drive to the hospital to pray for him.

"Absolutely!" we responded.

Upon arrival at the hospital, we were greeted and thanked by his mother. A nurse said we could go in and pray for him, but we had to whisper and could only apply anointing oil to his foot, so as not to arouse him.

So many emotions flooded our souls as we entered his room. We gently laid hands on his foot and began to pray.

As we did, we both felt what seemed like electricity running through our bodies and into his. The power of God was so real in that room.

A Higher Purpose

When we finished, we took his family out for dinner, prayed for them, and went home. We smiled and said, "This must have been God's purpose for what we went through in the failed adoption."

A few days later, the mother called to inform us that the day after we anointed her son and prayed for him, his brain swelling began to go down, his eye was completely restored, and there was absolutely no brain damage. We shouted at this miracle of God.

A few weeks later, the mother drove to our home and let us spend time with this miracle child, who had almost become our son. We realized more deeply than ever that God's thoughts are not ours.[1]

(A side note: In the years between the failed adoption and the call to come pray in the ICU, the Gardners were able to adopt a little girl. She is now a college student training to be a worship leader.)

chapter 34

MULTILEVEL FREEDOM

Sometimes Satan invades not just a person's mind but their body as well. That was certainly the case with the suffering woman whom Jesus delivered in Luke 13:10–13. The Scripture says she "had been crippled by a spirit for eighteen years. She was bent over and could not straighten up at all."

A contemporary parallel of this type of invasion took place in 2011, at Full Gospel Assembly, Hartford, Michigan, just as Pastor Shannon Truelove was finishing a Sunday night service. The sermon was over, and people were praying at the altar; various ones were requesting the laying on of hands for personal needs.

Just then, a man of the congregation came in the back door pushing a woman in a wheelchair—his ex-wife, in fact. They were still on good enough speaking terms that he was concerned about her decline over the past three months and wanted to get her some help. She had not been sleeping well; she claimed demons were trying to attack her; and she had lost her ability to walk.

As the man pushed her down the center aisle, the woman's voice started spewing out hostile remarks. "Get away from me, get away from me!" she bellowed, pointing toward the front of the church. Soon the pronouns changed from singular to plural. "We won't go! She belongs to us!"

This was not the first time the pastor had faced a demonic challenge. Turning to the worship team, he requested that they begin singing songs about the power of Jesus' blood. When the woman was close enough, he started praying for her deliverance. He sensed the Spirit guiding him to call out an evil spirit of rejection (tracing back to a hurtful father), then, a spirit of suicide, and finally, a spirit of infirmity.

Her body began to contort; she tumbled out of her wheelchair onto the floor. For some twenty minutes the deliverance battle went on. "We had to 'bind the strong man'[1] as Jesus said," the pastor notes, "and take authority over the various ways the Devil had tormented her throughout her life, mentally and physically."

Eventually, a breakthrough came. The woman sat up with a whole new demeanor on her face. She said her tormentors were all gone now. "I can even walk on my own!" she exclaimed—and proved it by walking out of the church that night under her own power. The wheelchair was no longer needed.

Since then, she continues to come to church and to enjoy good health. "She's in her right mind," Pastor Truelove reports, "and living in the freedom that God gives.

"The power of God is always stronger than the schemes of the evil one. The book of Revelation talks about how 'They triumphed over him by the blood of the Lamb and by the word of their testimony.'[2] That's why I had the worship team sing about the blood of Jesus. It holds the power to overcome any attack, sickness, disease, trial, or heartache the Devil throws at us."

Further, he mentions something interesting about the Isaiah prophecy that "no weapon forged against you will prevail, and you will refute every tongue that accuses you. This is the heritage of the servants of the LORD."[3]

"Notice—it doesn't promise that weapons won't be deployed against us. They certainly will from time to time. What the Scripture promises is that they will not *prevail.*

"The Christian life is not without attacks and hardships. However, we can walk in victory over every one of them."

chapter 35

CANCER, BEGONE

Paul Piffard, a real estate agent in Sarnia, Ontario, knows how to make complicated deals work. If you want to sell your property, even if it's not in perfect shape, he'll find people to at least come look at it. If you want to buy a house with a certain floor plan on a quiet street, he'll quickly show you several listings in your price range.

But in 2013, he ran up against a different kind of challenge he couldn't negotiate.

About four years ago, I doubled over in pain and ended up in the Emergency Room at the hospital. I was diagnosed with cancer. As they found out, I had a large tumor between my kidney and my bladder.

The cancer got worse, even after that tumor was removed. It went into my kidney, and I had my kidney removed. As time went on, I went in to have another checkup for cancer, and the doctor looked into my bladder this time. What he found there was very scary and frightening.

He turned the monitor toward me so I could see as I was lying on the examination table. He said, "I've got some really bad news for you. There are twenty-five large tumors inside your bladder, and they are aggressive. They need to be removed. As a matter of fact, we need to take out your bladder and your prostate, to be sure it doesn't come back again."

I was very scared and frightened at the time.

At this point, it is worth noting that Paul and his wife, Donna, "would welcome and seek prayer continually," says their pastor, Tim Gibb, at Bethel Pentecostal Church. "It was many times and many people praying," especially during a week of prayer in early January 2014. "We prayed for them at each prayer service."

My wife and I pressed in like we never had before. We started to seek the Giver of Life rather than the gift. We looked to the Healer and not the healing. And we worshiped God with all our heart and soul and strength. No matter what would happen, we would praise God.

When I went into surgery later that month, the doctor said, "We're going to look inside first." He put me out, so I knew nothing about what was going on. I expected that when I woke up, I would have no bladder and no prostate, and instead, a bag on the side of my body.

When I woke up, he was standing right there, and he said, "I have good news for you."

I asked, "What is it?"

He said, "You've been given another chance!" All the tumors had shrunk up and had gone into virtually nothing.

I am now cancer-free for over two years. I've been for four checkups. The Lord did a miracle in my life.

And I ask myself, *Why did he do it?* He did it so I could share with you his great love and mercy. I believe he can touch your life as well.

Pastor Gibb says, "The few weeks leading up to this scheduled surgery, this couple had made the deliberate decision to cast this problem on the Lord and to focus their full attention and trust on him. The story of King Jehoshaphat in 2 Chronicles 20 became their inspiration: 'Stand still and see the salvation of the LORD.'[1]

"As a result of this miracle, I have seen the Lord increase their compassion for others who are going through their own health crises. They speak words of faith and encouragement that God is still a healer today."

To watch Paul Pifford tell the story in his own words, go to vimeo.com/198779125.

AUDACIOUS

The start-up congregation had a robust vision back in 2010: to be "a Christ-centered, Bible-based, Spirit-empowered, multi-ethnic, trans-generational community of Christ-followers" on the south side of Sacramento, California.

But New Season Christian Worship Center didn't look very impressive there in a repurposed car showroom. The garage port doors were covered by curtains, but still, the acoustics were terrible. The air-conditioning couldn't seem to keep up, and parking was limited. Even so, the rent was high—almost too high for the congregation to manage, even while Pastor Samuel Rodriguez and his wife, Eva, made do on a half-salary.

One Sunday in 2013, Pastor Rodriguez was able to introduce a guest speaker from Texas named Cindy Jacobs, who happened to be making a West Coast swing. Along with her prepared message, she added a word of prophecy that sounded utterly crazy that day. "The Lord says that soon you will be owning *multiple* properties. And in addition, you will have a television network."

The pastor had to stifle a laugh. The little church had no media presence at all, not even a radio program. And here she was talking about not just a television program, but a whole *network*. Surely not.

On the drive home, Pastor Rodriguez looked at his wife and

said, "Well, I'm not doubting it, but … that was really an audacious prophecy." They both knew that if any of this was going to happen, it would have to be God's doing all the way.

Within eighteen months, the following events had bloomed:

1. The New Season congregation had grown financially strong enough to stop renting and to buy a church property with two buildings (containing two auditoriums) on five acres just off the busy South Sacramento Freeway.

2. An Assemblies of God church, located 140 miles northeast in Sparks, Nevada (Reno area), had been struggling to the point that the denomination called Pastor Rodriguez and offered the property (which included a sanctuary, a separate multipurpose building, spacious parking lots, and a parsonage) as a gift for a satellite campus. He had no hesitation in saying, "Yes! We'll take it. This is another fulfillment of what God said."

3. Solid plans were put in place for a twenty-four-hour TV network to be called "TBN Salsa," which would air nationwide in English to serve second- and third-generation Hispanic Americans. It launched on June 1, 2015, with a schedule that included not only Pastor Rodriguez's messages but also those of other Latino ministers and musicians.

Today, the Nevada church is flourishing with its own full-time campus pastor, utilizing satellite sermons from Sacramento. Another satellite campus has been opened fifty miles south in the Central Valley city of Stockton, California.

Pastor Rodriguez says, "There is a fine line between the pathetic and the prophetic. When an authentic word comes from heaven, it has the power to shift people, families, churches, and ministries from surviving to thriving!"

chapter 37

WHERE LEAST EXPECTED

The channels used by the Spirit to deploy his gifts don't always fit our assumptions. In this story, we get surprised by what happened to a retired pastor who began having major migraines. (The story is told by his friend and colleague, veteran Church of God Editor and Special-Projects Coordinator James E. Cossey.)

In January 2014, Charles Hollifield was stricken with severe migraine headaches, which surprised a leading neurologist at Erlanger Medical Center (Chattanooga, Tennessee), who stated that he had never seen a patient develop first-time migraines past age sixty. Doctors initially suspected a stroke or aneurysm. But all testing ruled those out and led to the diagnosis of chronic migraines.

Charles would be so affected by these debilitating headaches that he routinely got up staggering, holding his head, and writhing in agony. And at times, when he staggered and fell, he cut himself on various objects. Sometimes the pain was so severe that Mary, his wife, or one of their daughters found him passed out in the yard or on his shop floor. When they asked what had happened, he couldn't remember anything.

Over time, Charles became unable to drive, mow, operate power tools, or otherwise function normally. He would have Mary literally pack his head in ice for hours at a time, seeking for some semblance of relief.

Charles went through eight MRIs and five ultrasounds. The only help he could get was from injections into his scalp, which brought relief for just two or three days at a time. Through numerous doctor visits and three hospitalizations, he was told by three different neurologists, "We do not know of any cure for your condition."

Meanwhile, his church and family kept praying. People would come to the hospital and pray for God's intervention.

Charles had been an active minister and counselor in the Anchor Point Foundation, a local ministry for addicted and incarcerated men. On the afternoon of April 4, 2016, he made a bold—although at the time a seemingly foolish—decision. He knew his ministry partners were heading that afternoon to the Bradley County Corrections Center for a time of ministry. Charles decided he would go too. Though he had been unable to serve as in the past, he now said to Mary, "I may die today, but it won't be in this dark room. I'm going to the jail."

He got up and dressed. Driving erratically and in pain, he drove himself to the jail. When the singing finished, he staggered to the podium as if to preach, but instead addressed the chapel attendees by saying, "I am in pain. Some of you here know Jesus. You know how to pray. When you return to your cell, please pray for me."

He then turned and sat down so another minister could preach the sermon.

Interruption

As the minister began to speak, a young inmate, sitting near the back, stood and quietly walked over to Charles. The thin young man was covered in tattoos from his knuckles to his ears. The look on his face could only be described as vicious. Little did Charles realize at that moment that the "vicious look" was one of righteous indignation. This young inmate had been led to Christ through Anchor Point.

Stopping directly in front of Charles, the inmate (whose name turned out to be Charles as well) softly and quietly placed his palm on Charles Hollifield's forehead. In simple, childlike faith, he said, "Devil, this is the jail service! You don't belong here! You think you do, but you don't! We've turned this into a sanctuary!"

Then he continued, "I command you to take your hands off this man of God and leave this property." He then gave a word of thanks to God, turned, walked away, and sat again.

In that flash of a moment, Charles Hollifield's more-than-two-year battle with migraines ended. Instantly, the headaches ceased. Charles was healed by the power of God.

Sometime later, he visited his neurologist again. "Mr. Hollifield," the doctor began, "I am very sorry; there is still nothing we can do, except those injections that don't seem to work very well."

Charles interrupted him: "That's okay, Doc. I don't need you anymore, I've been to another physician, and I am *cured*!"

"Who is he?" the doctor inquired.

Charles spelled out the name of his new physician: "J-E-S-U-S."

Within a few minutes, the neurologist threw up his hands and said, "Praise the Lord!"

Reprise

Following the miracle healing, the young tattooed inmate was transferred from Bradley County to a state prison. On Saturday, June 3, 2017, Charles Hollifield drove to the facility to visit his inmate friend and brother in Christ. A strange and unusual thing happened on the way as Charles headed down the mountain and saw the state penitentiary coming into view. From out of nowhere, a severe migraine-like pain hit Charles in the back of his head—the first in fourteen months.

Without a thought, Charles reached up with one hand while driving with the other, touched his own head, and said, "Devil, you don't belong here! I am healed in the name of Jesus!"

The pain, which Charles estimates lasted no more than ten seconds, was gone instantly. Charles believes this was a satanic attack to try and discredit the miracle of April 2016 just as the two Charleses were about to be reunited to rejoice over it. There have been no other incidences like this before or since.

The next week, he made another visit to the neurologist. Once again, the two men left the examining room rejoicing over the healing power of Jesus.

God the Holy Spirit sometimes does the miraculous through some of the least likely individuals. Both Charles, the preacher, and Charles, the prisoner, rejoice over God's healing power. And, by the way, Charles, the prisoner, is now actively ministering in the state penitentiary, leading others to salvation, Holy Spirit baptism, and healing on a daily basis.

chapter 38

ADVANCE NOTICE

Seldom does God reveal what he has in mind for a person's distant future; usually we have to "walk by faith, not by sight."[1] One exception, of course, would be David the shepherd boy, who, while still a teenager, was anointed by a prophet to be Israel's future king. It didn't actually come to pass until he was thirty years old.

Something similar occurred the night in 2004, when Jon and Gwen Jennings, pastors of Fountain of Life Church in Phoenix, took their eleven-year-old son, Chris, to a large revival conference in a hotel ballroom. Dale Gentry, an evangelist with a strong prophetic anointing, called the boy out of the crowd and gave a short, simple word:

"I see you standing in front of thousands of young people leading worship."

The grade-school kid snickered. He had barely picked up a guitar at that point in his life or shown much interest in any kind of worship music.

His father says that when they returned home, "I purposely chose not to press the issue with my son. I waited to let the Lord work things out in his own timing."

A couple of years later, Chris started developing guitar skills and singing around the house. Soon his youth pastor asked him to lead a song for the weekly youth service. From that point onward, Chris began listening to worship music and participating at a deeper level in his youth group. By age sixteen, he was one of the guitar players on the church's main worship team, occasionally being asked to lead a song for the congregation. His parents still kept quiet about the prophetic word of the past.

However, in his latter high school years, Chris hit a faith wall and started to go off the rails spiritually. By his senior year, he was hanging around with atheist friends and questioning everything about God and faith.

"It was in that moment that the prophetic word from years earlier came back to me," says Pastor Jennings. "I told my wife that we, as his parents, had a responsibility to steward that prophetic word in prayer. Further, we were to position our son for his destiny, whenever the Father deemed the season right for fulfillment."

They sent Chris to a youth camp in Southern California, where he was invited to help lead worship. During those two weeks of camp, God showed up in his life. When he came home, he was a different young man. He had purpose and direction. Though still wrestling with his questions, he had encountered a living God.

In the fall of 2012, Chris enrolled at Grand Canyon University in Phoenix as a Christian studies major. There, he auditioned for the chapel worship team. His first year he played only the guitar, but by his junior year, he was chosen to be one of the chapel worship leaders. Everything was being brought full circle.

His parents attended the first chapel service Chris actually led. The GCU arena was packed with more than six thousand students. "As our son stepped to the microphone and led the student body in worship," Pastor Jennings says, "I turned to my wife and said, 'Do you remember the word he got at that revival meeting when he was eleven? It's being fulfilled right before our eyes!'"

When the service was over, the father hugged his son and asked if he remembered the word from long ago. He didn't. "But it didn't matter," the father says. "God had brought us through many challenging times and difficult seasons, intending all along to keep his promise in our son's life."

Today Chris Jennings is on staff at a large multi-site church in Chandler, Arizona, where he is the worship leader for students.

chapter 39

RIVER OF
THE SPIRIT

Sometimes when we think we've got life organized the way it should be, the Holy Spirit has to step in and upset the status quo.

Shortly after World War II, a number of denominations and networks came together and formed the PFNA—Pentecostal Fellowship of North America. Conventions were held, impassioned sermons were preached, and valuable contacts were made among the various groups.

The only problem—generally ignored—was that the group was all-white.

Yes, back at the Azusa Street Mission during the awakening of 1906 to 1909, many races had received the outpouring of the Spirit in the same building. Leading elder William J. Seymour was black. And eyewitness Frank Bartleman reported that, even in that Jim Crow era, "The color line was washed away in the Blood." But by mid-century, a lot of historical twists and turns had taken place, and lines had been drawn.

When Pentecostal Holiness Bishop Bernard E. Underwood was elected to head the PFNA in 1991, he set out to do something about this problem. He began dialogue with Bishop Ithiel Clemmons of the Church of God in Christ (COGIC), a large denomination of mostly African Americans. Four exploratory meetings of leaders were held over the next two years, leading up to a formal conference in the fall of 1994, to be called "Pentecostal Partners: A Reconciliation Strategy for 21st Century Ministry." The site was Memphis, headquarters of COGIC and, not incidentally, the city where a white man had gunned down Dr. Martin Luther King Jr. in the late 1960s.

Breakthrough

The moment never to be forgotten did not happen during one of the large evening sessions held in a downtown convention center and attended by more than three thousand. Instead, in an afternoon scholars' session on October 18, COGIC Bishop Charles E. Blake told the group with tears, "Brothers and sisters, I commit my love to you. There are problems down the road, but a strong commitment to love will overcome them all." At this, a spirit of weeping and repentance seemed to sweep the room. A young black man raised his voice in an utterance of tongues.

Immediately following this, the tall, thin form of Jack Hayford, well-known pastor of The Church on the Way (Van Nuys, CA) and prominent Foursquare Church leader, was seen striding toward the microphone to give the interpretation:

> For the Lord would speak to you this day, by the tongue, by the quickening of the Spirit, and he would say: My sons and my daughters, look, if you will, from the heavenward side of things, and see where you have been two separate streams—that is, streams as at flood tide. For I have poured out of my Spirit upon you and flooded you with grace in both your circles of gathering and fellowship.

But as streams at flood tide, nonetheless, the waters have been muddied to some degree. Those of desperate thirst have come nonetheless. For muddy water is better than none at all.

My sons and my daughters, if you will, look and see that there are some who have not come to drink because of what they have seen. You have not been aware of it, for only heaven has seen those who would doubt what flowed in your midst, because of the waters muddied, having been soiled by the clay of your humanness—not by your crudity, lucidity, or intentionality, but by the clay of your humanness the river has been made impure.

But look! Look, for I, by my Spirit, am flowing the two streams into one. And the two becoming one, if you can see from the heaven side of things, are being purified. And not only is there a new purity coming in your midst, but there will be multitudes more who will gather at this one mighty river, because they will see the purity of the reality of my love manifested in you. And so, know that as heaven observes and tells us what is taking place, there is reason to rejoice and to prepare yourself. For here shall be multitudes, more than ever before, coming to this joint surging of my grace among you, says the Lord.

God had made himself abundantly clear that change needed to happen.

The listeners were still absorbing this interpretation when Donald Evans,[1] a white Assemblies of God pastor from the South (Tampa, Florida), appeared holding a basin of water and a towel. He said the Lord had impressed him to wash the feet of a black leader as a sign of repentance. Soon he was kneeling in front of COGIC Bishop Clemmons, washing his feet and begging forgiveness for the sins of whites against their black brothers and sisters. The entire audience began to weep afresh.

The next thing to happen was COGIC Bishop Blake asking to wash the feet of Thomas Trask, general superintendent of the Assemblies of God. He said it was in repentance for any animosity blacks harbored against their white brothers and sisters.

The old die had been shattered; a new die was being cast. By the next afternoon's business session, the all-white PFNA had been dissolved, and a new constitution was underway for the PCCNA—Pentecostal/Charismatic Churches of North America—with full representation on its board and membership of denominations and groups regardless of color. In addition, a "Racial Reconciliation Manifesto" passed unanimously.[2]

Chairing the new board would be COGIC Bishop Clemmons, with his friend Bishop Underwood (Pentecostal Holiness) as vice-chairman. Also elected was Bishop Barbara Amos (Mount Sinai Holy Church of America), thus starting to bridge the gender gap as well.

The Results

In the years since the "Memphis Miracle," as it came to be called, when the old PFNA voted itself out of existence, membership has tripled from barely a dozen groups to more than thirty-six, including African American and Hispanic organizations, parachurch ministries, and megachurches. The association has expanded its vision from the United States and Canada to eagerly embrace its Mexican neighbors to the south as well.

Committed to a mission of "Demonstrating Unity in the Power of the Spirit," PCCNA denominational and church leaders agreed to accomplish more together than simply meet once a year and enjoy good fellowship. In the spirit of 1 John 3:18, which insists love is more than words, PCCNA members partnered with

World Vision[3] in the war against malaria. This parasitic disease still kills innocent children in developing countries, unlike the children of North America who are spared because of intentional intervention in the early twentieth century. United in vision and purpose, PCCNA member groups and ministries raised more than one million dollars for insecticide-treated bed nets to send to sub-Saharan Africa. Strategically distributed, along with important training for parents, malaria cases were reduced by over 50 percent where the nets were deployed. Many thousands of children are alive and well today because of the united PCCNA effort.

Other initiatives demonstrate the fresh unity of Pentecostal/charismatic streams flowing together into one river of the Spirit. Books published by PCCNA with contributions from a broad range of member groups inspire, teach, and bring hope. Various commissions encourage and equip leaders by exchanging best practices in the ministries of prayer, race relations, Christian unity, discipleship, communications and media, and women's ministries. Local chapters are emerging as citywide representations of the broader North American association.

The Holy Spirit's word that day in Memphis—"Look, if you will, from the heavenward side of things ... multitudes more who will gather at this one mighty river, because they will see the purity of the reality of my love ... here shall be multitudes, more than ever before coming to this joint surging of my grace among you,"—is being fulfilled. The stream of the Spirit that began flowing out of Azusa Street in 1906 has become a tsunami, unprecedented in its sweep across nations and races and peoples. PCCNA is humbled and honored to be living in that river.

WHAT CAN WE CONCLUDE?

What do we make of the inspiring reports we've just read? What do they signify? Four things come to mind:

1. **The Holy Spirit's gifts are not fading away.** They're still alive and well, flourishing wherever they are welcomed by God's people. They are not the private domain of any one denomination or network. The wind of the Spirit is blowing wherever it sees fit, and as vigorously today as ever.

2. **The Holy Spirit's gifts are active here on OUR continent in OUR time.** While thanksgiving is certainly in order for the miracle stories coming out of Africa, Asia, South America, and other parts of the world, this book focuses on our own continent: Canada, the United States, and Mexico. And not just stories from back in "the good old days" of previous revival. We have deliberately chosen examples of spiritual gifts in contemporary settings.

3. **The Holy Spirit "distributes [gifts] to each one, just as he determines"**[1] throughout the Body of Christ. Not just to a few. Not just to super-saints. Not just to those who are ordained. He is more than willing to use teenagers, new believers, ordinary moms and dads—anyone with faith to believe and the willingness to step out.

4. **Human problems, whether physical, emotional, financial, or spiritual, do not have to be permanent.** Rather, they can be the material in the hands of the Spirit for a miracle turnaround. Instead of saying, *O God, look how big is my mountain!* we can

say, *O mountain, look how big is my God!* The correct question is not, "How large is my problem?" It is, "How large is my God?"

We've called this book *Miracle Invasion* because there truly is a rising tide of supernatural breakthroughs across our continent and beyond. Jesus was not exaggerating when, on the night of the Last Supper, he said, "Whoever believes in me will do the works I have been doing, and they will do even greater things than these, because I am going to the Father."[2] A few weeks later, his disciples came down the steps from the upper room in the power of the Spirit and began to do just that. We can do the same!

The exercise of spiritual gifts is limited only by our hesitations. Jesus is the same today, in the twenty-first century, as he was in the first century. He is still confirming his gospel "by signs, wonders and various miracles, and by gifts of the Holy Spirit distributed according to his will."[3] We get the privilege of not just watching but *participating* in this great work.

Let us never lose faith in the message of Oliver Wells' faith-building song, "God Is Still Doing Great Things" (recorded by the Brooklyn Tabernacle Choir):

Are you standing in need of a miracle today?
Even doctors don't know what to do
God is able to make a way from no way
He's still able to carry you through

If we will just learn to trust and obey
We'd find that our Savior turns darkness into day
He alone can handle the challenges life brings
God is still doing great things …

If we let God's power work deep within
He's able to do more than we can comprehend
He alone can handle the challenges life brings
God is still doing great things.[4]

INDEX OF GIFTS

Throughout this book, the following gifts of the Spirit are demonstrated:

"Hard Case" (p. 67)
"Makeover in the Mall" (p. 78)
"'Twas Blind, but Now …" (p. 100)
"Wheelchair No More" (p. 106)
"A Promise Kept" (p. 122)
"A Miracle for Mom" (p. 132)
"Just Taking a Walk" (p. 139)
"Heartbreak, Then Healing" (p. 163)
"Cancer, Begone" (p. 169)
"Where Least Expected" (p. 174)

Miracles of Resurrection
"Up from a Watery Grave" (p. 13)
"Modern-Day Lazarus" (p. 83)
"'Wake Up, *Mija*!'" (p. 147)

Miracles (Other)
"The Lunch that Multiplied" (p. 41)
"Divine Arrest" (p. 97)

Tongues with Interpretation
"Northern Test" (p. 64)
"A Promise Kept" (p. 122)
"River of the Spirit" (p. 181)

Tongues—No Interpretation Needed
(Because the hearers already knew the original language)
"A Higher Code" (p. 24)
"The Message Gets Through" (p. 103)

Prophecy
"A Church in a Boxing Ring?" (p. 188)
"Double Trouble, Double Portion" (p. 115)
"When 'No' Became 'Yes'" (p. 127)
"Time to Uproot" (p. 142)
"Audacious" (p. 172)
"Advance Notice" (p. 178)

SOURCES

We wish to thank the following PCCNA groups (listed here alphabetically) for helping us locate the true stories in this book.

Assemblies of God

Formed: 1914
Headquarters: 1445 N. Boonville Ave., Springfield, MO 68502
Active mission work in 190 other nations
For more information: www.ag.org.

Local churches mentioned in this book:

p. 16—First Assembly Church, St. Peter, Missouri
p. 36—Ash Grove Assembly of God, Ash Grove, Missouri
p. 41—Calvary Church, Naperville, Illinois
p. 61—CT Church, Houston, Texas
p. 86—New Hope International Christian Center, Norwalk, California
p. 152—Gateway Christian Center, Tampa, Florida
p. 173—New Season Christian Worship Center/Cantico Nueva, Sacramento, California

Church of God

Formed: 1886
Headquarters: 2490 Keith St., NW, Cleveland, TN 37320
Active mission work in 182 other nations
For more information: www.churchofgod.org.

Local churches mentioned in this book:

p. 96—Carthage Family Worship Center, Carthage, Missouri
p. 163—Christ the Rock Church of God, Knoxville, Tennessee

See also p. 174—"Where Least Expected"

Church of God in Christ

Formed: 1897
Headquarters: 930 Mason St., Memphis, TN 38126
Active mission work in 60 other nations
For more information: www.cogic.org.

Local churches mentioned in this book:

p. 44—Sanctuary of Praise Church of God in Christ, Springfield, Missouri
p. 97—West Angeles Church of God in Christ, Los Angeles, California
p. 127—Outreach Church of God in Christ, Bremerton, Washington
p. 131—Greater Heights Church of God in Christ, Tacoma, Washington

See also p. 181—"River of the Spirit"

Church of God of Prophecy

Formed: 1903
Headquarters: PO Box 2910, Cleveland, TN 37320
Active mission work in 134 other nations
For more information: www.cogop.org.

Local churches mentioned in this book:

p. 103—Church of God of Prophecy, Kingsport, Tennessee
p. 126—Church of God of Prophecy, Douglasville, Georgia

Church of God of the Apostolic Faith

Formed: 1914
Headquarters: 399758 W. 3100 Road, Ramona, OK 74061
Active mission work in 6 other nations
For more information: www.cogaf.org.

Local church mentioned in this book:

p. 24—Forerunner House of Prayer, Green Forest, Arkansas

Coastal Church

Formed: 1994
Main address: 1160 West Georgia Street, Vancouver BC V6E 3H7
For more information: www.coastalchurch.org.

See also p. 132—"A Miracle for Mom"

Elim Fellowship

Formed: 1924
Headquarters: 1703 Dalton Road, Lima, NY 14485
Active mission work in 30 other nations
For more information: www.elimfellowship.org.

Local church mentioned in this book:

p. 144—Lighthouse Community Fellowship, South Butler, New York

Fellowship Network

Formed: 1962
Headquarters: 1000 N. Belt Line Road, Suite 201, Irving, TX 75061
For more information: www.thefellowshipnetwork.net.

Local church mentioned in this book:

p. 47—Believers Church, Douglasville, Georgia

The Foursquare Church

Formed: 1923
Headquarters: P.O. Box 26902, 1910 W. Sunset Blvd., Los Angeles, CA 90026
Active mission work in 145 other nations
For more information: www.foursquare.org.

Stories featuring Foursquare leaders in this book:

p. 30—"Detour?"
p. 181—"River of the Spirit"

Grupo Unidad

Formed: 1982
Headquarters: Blvd. Agua Caliente #11010, Col. Aviación, Tijuana, BC, Mexico 22420
For more information: www.unidad.org.

Local church mentioned in this book:

p. 88—Grupo Unidad, Tijuana, Baja California

Independent Assemblies of God International (Canada)

Formed: 1918
Headquarters: 330 Victoria Ave., PO Box 653, Chatham, ON N7M 5K8
For more information: www.iaogcan.com.

Local church mentioned in this book:

p. 158—Kangirsuk Full Gospel Church, Kangirsuk, Nunavik, Quebec

International Pentecostal Church of Christ

Formed: 1917
Headquarters: 2343 US Highway 42 Southwest, London, OH 43140
Active mission work in 18 other nations
For more information: www.ipcc.cc.

Local church mentioned in this book:

p. 166—Full Gospel Assembly, Hartford, Michigan

International Pentecostal Holiness Church

Formed by merger: 1911
Headquarters: PO Box 12609, Oklahoma City, OK 73157
Active mission work in 96 other nations
For more information: www.iphc.org.

Local church mentioned in this book:

p. 178—Fountain of Life, Elizabeth City, North Carolina

See also p. 181—"River of the Spirit"

National Hispanic Christian Leadership Conference

Formed: 2003
Headquarters: PO Box 293389, Sacramento, CA 95829
For more information: www.nhclc.org.

Local church mentioned in this book:

p. 173—New Season Christian Worship Center/Cantico Nueva, Sacramento, California

Open Bible Churches

Formed: 1935
Headquarters: 2020 Bell Ave., Des Moines, IA 50315
Active mission work in 45 other nations
For more information: www.openbible.org.

Local churches mentioned in this book:

p. 100—Living Word Open Bible Church, Cooper City, Florida
p. 147—New Life Open Bible Church, San Jacinto, California

See also:

p. 67—"Hard Case"
p. 115—"Double Trouble, Double Portion" regarding Eugene Bible College (now New Hope Christian College), Eugene, Oregon

Open Bible Faith Fellowship

Formed: 1982
Headquarters: 4490 7th Concession, Windsor, ON N9A 6J3
Active mission work in 15 other nations
For more information: www.obff.com.

Local church mentioned in this book:

p. 50—Windsor Christian Fellowship, Windsor, Ontario

Pentecostal Assemblies of Canada

Formed: 1919
Headquarters: 2450 Milltower Court, Mississauga, ON L5N 5Z6
Active mission work in 60 other nations
For more information: www.paoc.org.

Local church mentioned in this book:

p. 28, 170—Bethel Pentecostal Church, Sarnia, Ontario

See also p. 78—"Makeover in the Mall"

Pentecostal Church of God

Formed: 1919
Headquarters: 2501 Brown Trail, Bedford, TX 76095
Active mission work in 40 other nations
For more information: www.pcg.org.

Local church mentioned in this book:

p. 74—New Life Church, San Diego, California

See also the pastoral family featured in "Advance Notice" (p. 178)

United Evangelical Churches

Formed: 1958
Headquarters: PO Box 1000, San Juan Bautista, CA 95045
For more information: www.uecol.org.

See also p. 139—"Just Taking a Walk"

United Holy Church of America

Formed: 1894
Headquarters: 5104 Dunstan Road, Greensboro, NC 27405
Active mission work in 4 other nations
For more information: www.uhcainc.org.

Local churches mentioned in this book:

p. 136—Mount Zion Holiness Church of God, Galax, Virginia

NOTES

Setting the Stage

1 John 4:24.
2 Genesis 1:26.
3 Genesis 2:7.
4 1 Corinthians 2:14.
5 Acts 2; 8; 10; 19.
6 Acts 2.
7 1 Corinthians 2:11.
8 Genesis 21:15–20.
9 Exodus 3:2–5.
10 Acts 9:1–9.
11 Romans 12:6–8; 1 Corinthians 12:7–11; 1 Peter 4:10–11.
12 1 Thessalonians 5:23.
13 Acts 16:31.
14 Galatians 5:22–23.
15 Matthew 10:8.
16 Fuchsia Pickett, *Cultivating the Gifts and Fruit of the Holy Spirit* (Lake Mary, Fla.: Charisma House, 2004), 60.
17 Acts 2.
18 1 Corinthians 14:5.
19 Mark 16:17.
20 1 Corinthians 14:29–33.
21 1 Corinthians 14:13.
22 1 Corinthians 14:1.
23 1 Corinthians 14:31.
24 Ephesians 4:11; 1 Corinthians 12:28–29.
25 1 Corinthians 14:3 NKJV.

Chapter 1

1 1 Corinthians 12:9.
2 1 Corinthians 12:10.

Chapter 2

1 Romans 12:6.

Chapter 3

1 This church has since been renamed Forerunner House of Prayer. It is affiliated with the Church of God of the Apostolic Faith.
2 1 John 4:4.

Chapter 6

1 Pseudonym.
2 "Healing Is Here," copyright © 2012 Integrity's Praise Music (BMI) Deluge Music (BMI) (adm. at CapitolCMGPublishing.com) / Daniel Eric Groves Designee. All rights reserved. Used by permission.

Chapter 8

1 Currently renamed Sanctuary of Praise Church of God in Christ.
2 Pseudonym.

Chapter 11

1 Reprinted with permission from Don Nordin, *The Audacity of Prayer* (Lake Mary: Charisma House, 2014), 83–91.

Chapter 12

1 Currently renamed Water's Edge Church, as it sits only eight blocks from the shores of Lake Superior.

Chapter 13

1 Genesis 18:14 NKJV.
2 Romans 8:28 NKJV.
3 John 10:10.
4 3 John 2 NKJV.
5 Isaiah 53:5 KJV.
6 Matthew 10:8.

Chapter 14

1 Pseudonym.
2 Matthew 12:45.
3 Ephesians 4:27.

Chapter 15

1 Pseudonym.
2 Mark 8:22–25.
3 Luke 10:8–9.

Chapter 19

1 Adapted from the magazine article by Queen E. Phillips, "Under Arrest: A Modern-Day Miracle," *The Whole Truth*.

Chapter 21

1 1 Corinthians 14:9.

Chapter 22

1   Reprinted with permission from Tim Stafford, *Miracles* (Minneapolis: Bethany House Publishers, 2012) 11–19, 30–31, 218–19.

Chapter 23

1   Acts 5:29 MEV.
2   Job 42:10.
3   2 Kings 2.

Chapter 24

1   Psalm 27:7–8, 13–14 MEV.
2   Psalm 34:7 KJV.
3   2 Kings 19:35; Exodus 12:29–30.

Chapter 29

1   Ephesians 2:20.

Chapter 30

1   Psalm 22:3 WEB.

Chapter 32

1   www.arcticmissions.com.

Chapter 33

1   Reprinted with permission from Steve Gardner, "His Ways!" *Church of God Evangel,* May 2015, 16.

Chapter 34

1   Mark 3:27 KJV.
2   Revelation 12:11.
3   Isaiah 54:17

Chapter 35

1   2 Chronicles 20:17 NKJV.

Chapter 38

1   2 Corinthians 5:7.

Chapter 39

1   See also "The Spiritual Rookie" story.
2   http://pccna.org/documents/1994manifesto.pdf.
3   https://www.worldvision.org.

Conclusion

1   1 Corinthians 12:11.
2   John 14:12.
3   Hebrews 2:.4
4   "Still Doing Great Things," © 2002 Wello Music/ASCAP. Recorded on the Brooklyn Tabernacle Choir's *Be Glad* album.